MORE FA~~STER BACK~~WARDS

Rebuilding David B

Christine Smith

To Dennis —
May you always
follow
your
dreams!

— Chris—
1/29/2013

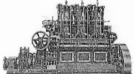

OLD HEAVY DUTY PUBLISHING

More Faster Backwards: Rebuilding David B

Copyright © 2012 by Christine Smith

Old Heavy Duty Publishing
PO Box 1431
Bellingham, WA. 98227

MoreFasterBackwards.com

Cover Art by Rebecca West

Graphics by Jeffrey Smith

ISBN-13: 978-0-615-54089-4
Library of Congress Control Number 2011919023

Printed in the United States of America

Dedication

To those who believe in themselves and have the strength to follow their dreams.

&

To all of my friends and family who came to help.

CONTENTS

Acknowledgements

THANKFUL ACKNOWLEDGMENT to everyone who helped in the reconstruction of the *David B*, the starting of our business, and the writing of this book. In particular I'd like to recognize: Grant Bird, Sean Bull, Marla Cilley, Andy and Jenny Cowan, Bill Dodson, Bonnie Gauthier, Jake Hartsoch, Lisa Hawkins, Rick Isackson, Dave Jackson, Loren Kapp, Christy Karras, Dan Krivonak, Greg Krivonak, Annie Leonard-Shannahan, Tim Mehrer, Aaron Mynatt, Jack Mynatt, Michael Naselow, Annie Patrick, Dan Pease, Abby Polus, Terry Richard, Phil Riise, Tom Riley, Drew Schmidt, Jon-Paul Shannahan, Ann Smith, Kirk Smith, Jeremy Snapp, Michael Start, Keith Sternberg, Barbee Teasley, Cynthia Topp, Cathy Wade, Rebecca West, Bruce Williams, Bob Woody, Carol Woody, Leigh Woody, Steve Woody, Pam Young.

IN MEMORY of Ian Mynatt, Fran Stevens-Woody, and Dan Zimmerman, who's contributions to the *David B* will always be with us.

MOST OF ALL thank you to Jeffrey Smith who is my constant love and companion.

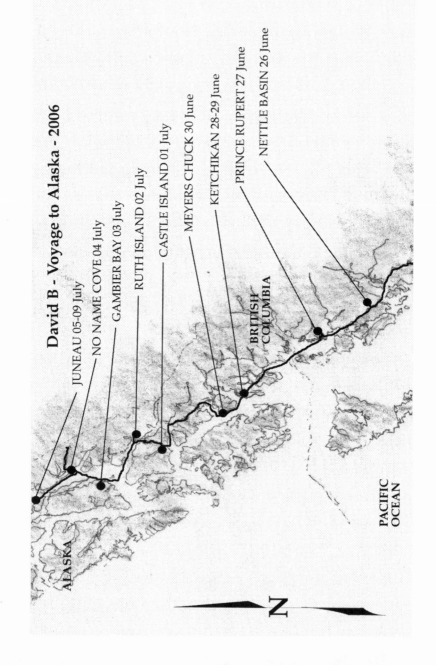

David B - Voyage to Alaska - 2006

JUNEAU 05-09 July
NO NAME COVE 04 July
GAMBIER BAY 03 July
RUTH ISLAND 02 July
CASTLE ISLAND 01 July
MEYERS CHUCK 30 June
KETCHIKAN 28-29 June
PRINCE RUPERT 27 June
NETTLE BASIN 26 June

ALASKA

BRITISH COLUMBIA

PACIFIC OCEAN

N

viii

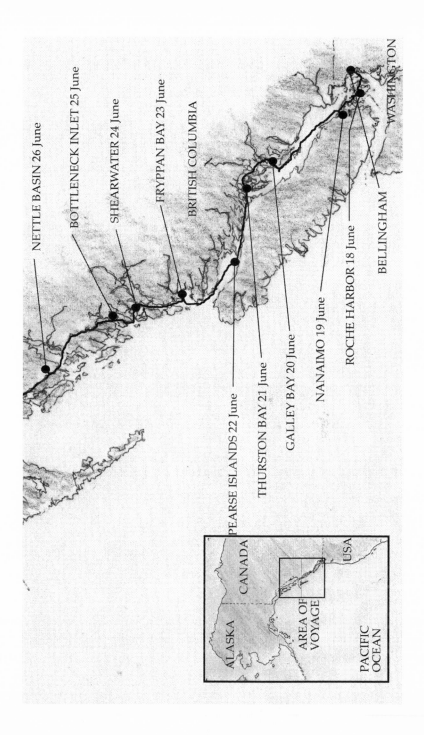

NETTLE BASIN 26 June

BOTTLENECK INLET 25 June

SHEARWATER 24 June

FRYPPAN BAY 23 June

BRITISH COLUMBIA

PEARSE ISLANDS 22 June

THURSTON BAY 21 June

GALLEY BAY 20 June

NANAIMO 19 June

ROCHE HARBOR 18 June

BELLINGHAM

WASHINGTON

ALASKA

CANADA

AREA OF
VOYAGE

USA

PACIFIC
OCEAN

ix

To be truly challenging, a voyage, like a life, must rest on a firm foundation of financial unrest. Otherwise you are doomed to a routine traverse, the kind known to yachtsmen, who play with their boats at sea—"cruising" it is called. Voyaging belongs to seamen, and to the wanderers of the world. who cannot, or will not, fit in. If you are contemplating a voyage and have the means, abandon the adventure until your fortunes change. Only then will you know what the sea is all about . . .

Which shall it be: bankruptcy of purse or bankruptcy of life?

~Sterling Hayden

Chapter 1

THERE'S A COLLECTION OF OLD
MEN ON THE DOCK

M/V David B -- Ship's Log				Date	18 June 2006	
Time	Location	Wind	Baro	Depth	Remarks	
0945	UNDERWAY BELLINGHAM					
1430	ANCHORED ROCHE H			32 FT	CLEAR	
2230	WIND S ~ E	c r				

IT WAS JUST OVER EIGHT YEARS since we first saw her. In fact, it was eight years, nineteen days and a handful of hours since she became ours. Jeffrey stood in the doorway of the pilothouse. "Ready for the bowline," he said with a grin.

My stomach was nervous with excitement and apprehension as I waited for Jeffrey to say those words. The *David B* was heading back to Alaska for the first time since she was launched in 1929. Only this time, we were taking her to Juneau to carry passengers.

I looked at the collection of old men drawn to the *David B* while she waited to get underway. It was the sound of the boat's antique engine that brought them here. It happens every time. "Ka-Pow!" The ancient engine starts. "Ching-ching-ching . . . Ching-

ching-ching." It begins its mechanical waltz, then a few smoke rings rise from the stack, and *poof*—old men seem to spontaneously generate out of thin air. Most days when they come, they come armed with questions about cylinders, injectors, stroke and bore, gears, RPM and horsepower. More often, they come to reminisce about their youth.

"How many cylinders ya got there?" one of the men asked Jeffrey as he walked up.

"Three cylinders, with a gear." Jeffrey smiled from his perch in the pilothouse. The *David B's* reverse gear is always a surprise to the old-timers who grew up with engines that could not go into reverse without first shutting down.

Jeffrey continued to answer questions while Sean and I worked together to untie the lines holding the *David B* to the dock.

"Excuse me," I said to the man, who had now parked himself in front of the boarding gate. He moved out of the way and continued to ask Jeffrey about the boat's engine.

Aaron, our engineer and business partner, was standing on the back deck with a fender. He looked up at the stack and noted the color of the smoke. He was nervous but stood leaning suavely on his fender, looking good in his sunglasses, Bowling Green University Ski Team sweatshirt, and slightly baggy shorts. His girlfriend, Havilah, was on board, and I think he wanted to make a good impression.

I'm not sure we'd have the boat today if it weren't for Aaron. As a twenty-something, he'd sacrificed a lot for the boat, the least of which was living in our eight-hundred-square-foot house with us, married people in their mid-thirties.

Aaron had inherited some money from his grandfather, and with encouragement from his parents, he'd invested it in the *David B*. In the year and a half he had been living with us, he had won our hearts with his humor, hard work, and sleep habits. We'd asked a lot of this twenty-four-year old, and he had always kept up with the pace. I watched him for a minute, jealous that his medium build could still metabolize a six-pack of beer and bag of Cheetos with no obvious effect.

I shifted my gaze from Aaron to Sean, who was on the foredeck gathering up the dock lines and putting them away. He had been working for us as a shipwright for the last six months to help get the *David B* ready for this trip, and now that the carpentry was done, he was ready to help out as Mate. I turned around to close the gate and smiled at the man on the dock. He stepped back from the boat and stood still with his arms limp at his sides. He smiled back at me with a distant look in his eyes. I wondered what long-ago memories the sound of the *David B's* engine sparked in him. When he was young, the harbor would have been filled with the distinct sounds of engines from Washington Iron Works, Atlas-Imperial, Enterprise, and Fairbanks-Morse. I sighed to myself at the sight of the slightly overweight, flannel-clad man on the dock as he listened to the *David B's* 3-cylinder Washington-Estep.

"Ka-snap" and a long "shhhhhhhhh" of compressed air came from the engine room as Jeffrey shifted the *David B* into reverse. Slowly, we slid away from the dock.

Jeffrey spun the big wooden wheel and gently pushed the long-handled brass shifter forward. Another rush of compressed air: "sushhhh."

I looked back at Aaron and then to the row of fiberglass yachts behind us. The aft end of the *David B's* big black wooden hull neared them. Aaron shifted his stance and readied his two-foot-long rubber fender, which seemed ridiculously small to fend our 135,000-pound boat off from the shiny white fiberglass yacht directly behind us.

Jeffrey worked to maneuver the *David B* out of her slip by shifting in and out of gear. I gathered the lines from the back deck, smiled nervously at Aaron, then went forward, stopping for a moment at the pilothouse door to watch Jeffrey as he cajoled the *David B* back and forth. Between each bump of power, he let the boat coast just a bit, all the while taking in the feel of her momentum. Jeffrey worked the boat with the skill of a lover. Every movement she made, he watched carefully to see how she responded to his commands, the light breeze, and the incoming tide.

The sun was shining into the pilothouse and onto Jeffrey's tall, thin runner's body as he maneuvered the boat from our tight slip. I watched him pause, turn around, and crouch down to look out the back windows. It was a beautiful dance to watch. He loved this boat, and whatever he asked her to do, she loved him back with a predictable response that showed how much they already understood each other. We cleared the row of yachts behind us, and Jeffrey straightened up the *David B*. As we headed out of the harbor, people stood on their decks waving and cheering us on. A couple horns sounded in congratulations. Jeffrey sounded back. These people knew us, and they knew how long and how hard we had worked on the *David B* to get to this day. We rounded the breakwater and entered Bellingham Bay.

It was Sunday, a good day to start a journey. We had carefully planned to avoid leaving on a Friday since it is bad luck, and Sean, who's well versed in the superstitions of sailors, was pleased with our decision. He had helped increase our good luck for a safe journey the night before by rearranging the mugs hanging in the galley to make sure they were all facing the proper way, banishing bananas, and informing us that both whistling and cutting our fingernails into the water were strictly forbidden.

Although it was a warm June day, it felt good to stand in the galley next to the warmth of the crackling wood-fired cookstove while I organized the pots and pans. On the bridge deck, Jeffrey and Sean discussed the long list of projects that needed to be completed while we were underway. Aaron passed me on his way down to the engine room. He needed to do his top-of-the-hour engine check. It had been roughly thirty years since the engine had been run regularly, and we didn't know any of its habits. With that in mind, Aaron's plan was to check the engine's temperature every fifteen minutes and oil all seventy-two moving parts on the outside of the old Washington every other hour. He had been down there long enough for me to forget about him, and we weren't much farther than Eliza Island when he came up out of the engine room with his forehead creased.

"Dude," Aaron interrupted the guys. "Something's up with the thrust bearing. I don't know what's going on, but the temp's going though the roof. It's a hundred and eighty degrees. We need to shut down pronto."

Jeffrey looked at him with unbelieving eyes and stopped talking for a moment. "It was working fine last week when we went out to Sucia," he finally said. "What's different? Did you forget anything when you started the engine?"

Aaron shook his head. "No, I can't think of what I could have missed." He turned and stared out the window.

Maybe, I thought to myself, if Aaron stares long enough out the window, the answer will come jumping out of the water and land flopping on the deck, making everything all right. A loud ticking sound began to amplify from the engine directly below our feet.

"What's the oil level in the Manzel?" Jeffrey asked.

Aaron straightened up. "I don't know."

"Go down to the engine room and slow us down so I can take the boat out of gear, then let's check the Manzel's oil level," Jeffrey said in a calm tone.

Aaron disappeared down the ladder. There was no throttle in the pilothouse, so it was Aaron's job to control the speed of the engine. When the engine slowed down to 175 rpm or so, Jeffrey shifted into neutral and joined Aaron down below.

I stepped up to the bridge deck and glanced at Sean. "I hope this isn't serious," I said.

"I think it will be all right. Like Jeffrey said, the engine worked fine last week. I'm sure the bearing just needs more oil." Sean shrugged. "Problems are going to come up with that engine, and when they do, Jeffrey and Aaron are going to fix them." He leaned forward and held on to the wheel.

"I know you're right, but I'd hoped we'd get a little farther down the road before shit started breaking. We're only forty-five minutes into a six-week cruise, and Juneau is looking a long way away right now."

I consoled myself with the view out the window. Gulls and Caspian Terns wheeled overhead in search of small fish in the sparkling blue water. A seal watched us briefly, then slid quietly beneath the surface. "I'm just worried," I confided to Sean, "that we won't make it in time to meet up with our first-ever real passengers."

Jeffrey's voice, with its slight Midwest accent, rose above the idling engine. I couldn't quite hear his words, but his tone sounded calm. It was a good sign. Then Aaron's deeper voice boomed up though the deck. "Well, fuck me! I thought it filled itself."

Sean smiled. "They evidently figured something out."

Jeffrey emerged from the engine room and stepped up onto the bridge deck. I watched him draw a deep breath before taking the wheel. My eyes were glued on him. The muscles in his jaw were tight. I waited for him to say something. He lifted his right hand to the brass gear shifter and held on to it, then scanned the pilothouse. "I can't believe that he thought that Manzel just filled itself with oil. If he'd put together a checklist, he'd have known to fill the damned thing up." Slowly he pushed the handle forward. "The Manzel was empty. Nothing was getting any oil. We almost burned up the thrust bearing and who knows what else. Fuck, that was a close call." Jeffrey held on to the shifter until the engine clicked into gear. "I've got to get him to make a checklist, but he's just not interested."

In a few minutes Aaron came up, smiling. The temperature for the thrust bearing had come down to 121 degrees now that the Manzel high-pressure oiler had oil. He grabbed a bag of Cheetos and started munching.

"You've gotta get a checklist. It's just too hard to remember everything in your head," Jeffrey said as Aaron offered up some Cheetos.

"I know. I know. I'll start working on one. There just hasn't been any time," Aaron countered with his mouth full. "I've got a little time before my next engine-room check, so I'll be out on deck with Havilah."

"There's just so much that can go wrong," Jeffrey said, taking a handful of Cheetos before Aaron left. "We can't afford to screw up even a little bit. We've spent so much time bringing this boat back, we just *can't* fuck it up. Think of all the years of work we've put into it."

The first time we were shown the *David B*, I thought it was a mistake. I stood on her deck listening to Jeffrey talk to the boat's owner as if he were interested in buying the rotten old thing. Honestly, I just thought Jeffrey was being nice.

"Rough" was a polite way of describing the *David B's* condition. Her hull was black and weathered, with planks that were pitted, and her paint was peeling. The billboard, which protects the bow from the anchor, was rotting, with some of its vertical staves broken or missing, and the white pilothouse sat old and faded on the aft end of the deck like a forgotten old woman in her rocking chair.

We had first gotten the idea to rebuild a boat during a phone call Jeffrey had made to his friend Michael, whom he had known from his early days of working on the big schooners in Maine. Michael was sort of Jeffrey's maritime confidant. Before then, Jeffrey and I had tried to raise money to build a new schooner. Jeffrey spent countless hours drafting the plans for this sailboat. She was to be named *Ceremony*. We put together an IPO and raised a little money, but that whole plan fell apart in 2001 when the stock market tumbled. Still, we wanted to run a passenger boat of our own, so we began to look for other options.

"Guess what?" Jeffrey said one evening after calling Michael to catch up on the gossip in Maine.

"I don't know. What?" I sat back in my old hand-me-down green office chair.

"Michael just gave me the phone number of a guy out on Lopez Island who might be able to help us find a boat." Jeffrey's eyes sparkled. "His name's Jeremy, and he evidently knows a shit-ton about old wooden boats and has a couple for sale. With the right-shaped hull we could re-rig it as a schooner." The words were coming out of Jeffrey so fast I could hardly follow along. "We could redo the interior and set it up with private cabins to make the boat exactly how we want it."

"How long do you think it would take to rebuild a boat and have it up and running?" I asked, wondering if this was the answer to our dream.

"I think we could do it in two years." Jeffrey said without too much thought.

We spent the rest of the night talking eagerly about the prospect of finding a boat. Why had we not thought about this before?

"I wish we had done this instead of trying to build a boat," I said.

"Yeah, maybe, but I still want to build *Ceremony* one day." Jeffrey had a sadness in his voice.

"I know. I do too, but I wish we hadn't gone eight thousand dollars into debt to pay a group of lawyers and accountants to produce a pile of paperwork for an IPO." I knew this was a touchy subject. We had failed with the *Ceremony* IPO and we would be paying for it for a very long time.

"I feel sort of ripped off by that. Why does it have to be so impossible for people like us to get ahead?" Jeffrey said wistfully. "The system seems to be only for people who already have money, and neither one of us seems to be able earn enough to do what we want."

"Well, Jeffrey, what's done is done. We should leave *Ceremony* behind for a while and move forward with this new plan." I stared at the blueprint of the *Ceremony* above Jeffrey's desk. "She would have been beautiful if we could have pulled it off." It hurt me to see all the work Jeffrey had put into her.

"Yeah, she would have been. Maybe we can build her some other time," Jeffrey answered.

"Yeah, maybe." I knew *Ceremony* was just a dream and probably always would be.

The new plan, however, was coming together fast. Jeffrey was going to call Jeremy the next morning to glean some information about his boats. If he had one we liked, we could use our business plan for *Ceremony* and change it to fit with whatever boat we found. Buying an old boat to refurbish was our new path, and I went to bed with dreams of entertaining and cooking on a boat that sailed through the San Juan Islands—so much more fun than my job as a receptionist and shipper for a small new-age record label.

I spent the next day at work packaging up music CDs and answering phones. While I worked, I daydreamed about our future boat and the people who would come with us. I dreamt up gourmet recipes I would cook for them, and I imagined the whales that would swim around the boat to the delight of our passengers. As much as I enjoyed working for Soundings of the Planet, I felt numb. There wasn't any creativity in putting CDs into padded envelopes. Soundings was someone else's dream. I wanted my own.

Jeffrey called around lunch time. "So, I talked with Jeremy. He wants to meet with us this weekend to show us his boats. We'll need to catch the one p.m. ferry to Lopez Island."

I felt my spirit lift with the hope of finding a boat and to hear Jeffrey so excited. Soon after the IPO for the *Ceremony* had failed, Jeffrey had become directionless. It was sad to see him frustrated with where his life was going.

"I was thinking," he continued, "that it might be fun to walk the docks tonight after work where the fishing boats are tied up so we can see what's for sale right here in town."

"That sounds fun. I'll hurry home." I hung up after a few more words and couldn't wait to get off work.

Later that evening we drove to Squalicum Harbor's Gate 5, where the remnants of the once-bustling Bellingham fishing fleet are moored. The parking lot had a congregation of old beater pickup trucks and trailers containing enormous mounds of fishing nets. There was a kind of empty chill I felt as we drove past the nets. They looked like they had been sitting there a long time, waiting for some far-off day when the great runs of salmon would return. Some of the mounds had blue tarps protecting them from the weather, but most just sat out in the open.

After we parked the car, we strolled down the ramp to see the boats. The fishing fleet was old, some boats from as early as the 1920s. Each boat seemed to have a personality and an old-timer's knowledge of tides, currents, weather, and the ways of fish, stored like pages of an encyclopedia between untold of layers of paint. We stopped at the *Leith W.* It had a For Sale sign on it: $50,000.

"She's pretty," I said as Jeffrey sized up the boat.

"And in the right price range, too. If Jeremy's boats don't work out, then we can take a better look at this one." Jeffrey walked down the dock alongside the *Leith W.*

"It's nice to feel like we have some options," I said later as we headed for home. "I can't wait to check out Jeremy's boats."

I love to ride the ferry. There's always an interesting mix of islanders and tourists to watch. While I waited for Jeffrey to return to our seats from the on-board cafeteria, I listened to the clacking sound of cars being loaded on to the vehicle deck below. The vibration of the ferry as it powered ahead in its berth was soothing to my nervous energy. Outside, a couple gulls stood on a piling, one with its mouth wide open and its head bowed to announce the arrival of another.

When we got off the ferry, Jeremy was there waiting. He reminded me of an oversized leprechaun and was dressed straight out of the Dust Bowl with a wool vest over the top of a flannel shirt, dirty black jeans, and a newsboy cap. He looked to be in his late forties.

It was a short drive to the first boat he wanted to show us. We turned left and drove down a private road, past a couple of old buildings. The road ended at an abandoned rock quarry near the shore.

There were two old boats anchored twenty or so feet off the beach, the *Yakatat* and the *David B*. We walked toward the rock-lined shore where the quarry's operations had apparently taken place. Dandelions and buttercups poked through the rocks. There was no dock to get out to the boats, so Jeremy had rigged up a long float that swung from the boats to the shore. It looked sketchy, built with some two-by-fours, plywood, Styrofoam and a little bit of non-skid taped to the surface for safety.

"I have to be careful not to leave the float up against the beach," Jeremy said as he grabbed hold of a line and began hauling in the float. "You see, if you're working out on the boats and the tide starts going out, the float will fetch up on the rocks." He kept pulling on the line and the float slowly began to pivot. "When we get over to the other side, we'll pull the float back out. It's a bear to get the thing off the rocks if it gets stuck. Even worse, if the tide is really low, it can break the float." Jeffrey and I nodded that we understood how important it was to keep the float off the beach.

Jeremy led the way with a slight skip in his step. I carefully stepped on after Jeffrey, and the combined weight of the three of us caused the float to sag so that the top was even with the water. Any more weight and it would have been partially submerged.

I looked down and saw some sea stars grazing on the intertidal rocks. As I got over deeper water, I could see anemones and mussels that clung under the middle of the float. The visibility was good, and I wished I could lie down on my belly and spend the day watching the fish that swam under the float. I stepped off the swing float and onto another set of floats tied to the decaying *David B*.

Maybe I was hearing the conversation wrong, but as I followed Jeffrey onto the *David B*, it became clear that Jeremy wasn't interested in selling the *Yakatat*. She was in better condition. It was the *David B* he was trying to get rid of. The voice in my head kept saying, *This can't be the boat we're here to see. It's so old and rotten. There's no way we can take this project on. It's just too big.* I stood on deck trying to take it all in while Jeremy did his best to talk up the finer points of the *David B*.

"What's underneath the plywood?" Jeffrey asked as he examined the deck, which was covered in a thick layer of black tar. It was ugly but radiated pleasing warmth from the heat of the sun.

"There's two-and-a-quarter-inch decking under there." Jeremy said with his hands thrust deep into his pockets as he rocked back on his heels. "The deck's a little soft in places, so I put the plywood down, and then once a year I give it a good coat of tar to kinda hold everything together."

I looked down at the deck as he talked, not really knowing what to think or say and feeling a little disappointed. This boat was beyond anything I knew, but I trusted Jeffrey's judgment, and he seemed to be asking thoughtful questions.

Jeremy, I noticed, was not very neat in his tarring, as there were tar splatters up the side of the bulwarks and on the forward break beam. With my eyes, I followed the splatters to the foredeck. At the bow, the stem rose about a foot and a half above the deck. I didn't know it at the time, but it was unusual for the stem to be sticking out of the foredeck like that. There should have been bulwarks attached to it. Just behind the stem there were two holes in the deck where the anchor chain came up, but the windlass that hauls the chain was missing and the empty space where it should have been was covered with more tar-soaked plywood. On the port side of the foredeck, a big rusty pipe stuck out of the deck, and just inboard of the pipe on the centerline was a mast. A spider's web connected the two, and it swayed lightly in the soft breeze, its occupant curled up somewhere out of sight. Not far from the mast was the scuttle leading down to the interior of the boat. It seemed odd, but for some reason it didn't have any doors.

What a wreck. I wondered if this was a good idea, but I continued my survey of the boat while Jeffrey talked with Jeremy.

Where the plywood and tar decking met the outside edges of the boat, a "new" covering board had been added to protect the frame ends from rainwater. It was unfinished and looked as if a careless beaver had chewed out the curve that was supposed to channel rainwater off the foredeck. I imagined that in a big downpour, the water would run down the covering board and off the foredeck in rapids instead of a smooth sheet of water. Even through the covering board was clearly unfinished, it, too, had multiple layers of tar, and the "chew" marks added to the *David B's* overall ambience of old age and decay.

At the aft edge of the foredeck there was an eighteen-inch step down to the main deck where the three of us stood around a large hatch. Its removable cover was a hacked-together plywood lid with a good dousing of tar. Jeremy kept the lid propped open a few inches to allow fresh air into the belly of the boat.

Jeffrey asked him, "So, what did you do with the boat?"

"Well, I was going to do some fish-buying with it. I built pens down below that I thought I'd use for storing fish, but I never got around to it," Jeremy explained. "I've mostly done some mooring-stone setting with the boat. The last time I tried to set one, it turned out to be too heavy and the windlass went right though the deck." He pointed toward the beach. "It's over there now."

This was Jeffrey's show, and while I agreed that buying an old boat was what we should do, I had no prior interest in or much knowledge about boats. We hadn't really talked much about the care and ownership of an old wooden boat; we just suddenly had an extremely large bee in our bonnets to get one. Sure, Jeffrey had worked on wood boats and even built a small one himself, but this boat was big, built in 1929 and showing her age.

As I contemplated this old boat, I was reminded of my great-grandmother, old and wrinkled, sitting proud and silent waiting for someone to ask her about her story. The pilothouse, like the rest of the boat, was in need of care. The *David B's* windows had the faraway expression of an old woman who'd seen much hardship and was tired of living. Maybe the soul of the *David B* entertained the idea of slowly sinking into the waters here in Shoal Bay and resting its tired keel on the rocks just below.

Not too long ago, a boat in the condition of the *David B* would have been burned on the beach in a spectacular funeral pyre. Today, old wood boats are dismantled with chainsaws and heavy equipment, their toxic remains unceremoniously discarded into dumpsters and then hauled off to landfills.

The boat rocked a bit as Jeffrey and Jeremy walked to the back end of the pilothouse. I took off my backpack and dug out my camera. It was warm on deck, so I lingered with my camera to take pictures and to soak up some sunshine.

I walked the opposite direction from Jeffrey and Jeremy over to the doorless scuttle and leaned my head into the dark interior of the boat. It smelled old, like a mildewy canvas tent. As my eyes adjusted to the dark, I could see that the area called the fo'c'sle had mounds of junk piled up everywhere. There were heavy lines, cast-iron things, mattresses, fifty-five-gallon drums, oversized handmade wrenches, a potbelly woodstove, and a host of other items hiding in the shadows. There were some bunks that were crammed full with the majority of this collection of crap. I climbed down the ladder to get a better look.

The overhead and the inner hull planking, known confusingly as the ceiling planking, were painted white, the flooring a dark red. It had a very nautical feel to it, in an old-fashioned sort of way. The fo'c'sle, like the foredeck, was marked at the aft end by a step down. There was a bulkhead made up of two layers of diagonal tongue–and-groove with a heavy door separating the fo'c'sle from the middle of the boat and the area that Jeremy had called the fish hold.

The entrance to the fish hold from the fo'c'sle was guarded by two fifty-five-gallon drums that had been laid down against the boat's fuel tanks. I snapped a few pictures and then squeezed past the drums. On either side of the boat were the two fish pens that Jeremy had built but had never gotten around to using. The fish hold opened up like a cavern. It was dark, with a thin stream of sunlight coming through the hatch.

I scanned the underside of the original deck planking that from the topside was obscured by plywood and tar. The planking was old, weathered and in places rotten, but some of the beautiful tight, vertical-grained Douglas fir still remained firm. These planks were laid down almost seventy years ago, when people thought that the old-growth trees of the Pacific Northwest were an inexhaustible resource. People like my great-grandfather had flocked to the Northwest to make their fortunes cutting down the enormous slow-growing monarchs of the forest that made up the *David B* and other boats like her.

I continued my tour of the interior of the boat. Just aft of the fish pens was another bulkhead. This one was newer and made of plywood. It appeared to have been constructed by Jeremy. At the bottom center of the bulkhead he had attached a wok, like you would use to make a stir-fry. It was odd and a bit puzzling, but as I leaned in to investigate, I saw that the wok covered up some part of the engine that was sticking out through the bulkhead.

Jeffrey and Jeremy were talking in the engine room just behind the bulkhead with the wok. I went though the doorway and stopped to look at the engine. It was big and green, the size of a Volkswagen. In the low light, it seemed more sculpture than late-1920s state-of-the-art technology. It stood about six feet tall. On the outside was a confusing array of pipes, rods, and tiny copper lines. I slid up next to Jeffrey, who was asking rapid-fire questions. The conversation was over my head, and their voices quickly faded away, like the voices of adults in a Peanuts cartoon. While I took pictures, Jeffrey eventually exhausted his questions about the engine and left with Jeremy to continue his tour into the fish hold.

For a moment I was alone in the near dark with just the single light bulb casting shadows around the edges of the engine room. I bent down to read the company name cast into the engine's inspection plates: Washington Iron Works. The name sounded strong and conjured up images of molten metal and exploding sparks. I stood back up and leaned against the tool bench. This boat had Jeffrey written all over it. He loved old things and old technology. I smiled to myself, and in that moment I knew in my heart that this boat was ours. It wasn't so much a voice in my head as it was a grip around my heart. I sometimes like to pretend that it was at this moment that the boat picked us to save it from its long years of neglect and decline. I left the engine room ready to see Jeremy's other boat, knowing already that we had found our future here with the *David B*.

"Hey guys, does it feel like we're slowing down?" Jeffrey asked not long after he and Aaron fixed the problem with the thrust bearing.

"What?" I said, startled, as his voice pulled me back from the past.

"Hey, take the wheel for a moment," Jeffrey told Sean and raced down to the engine room.

"What do you think's going on?" I asked Sean. He pressed his lips together and raised his shoulders. "I don't know. Maybe you should ask your engineer."

Aaron was on deck, sleeping like a princess. I felt my stomach tighten and wished we had a normal boat with a normal engine. The kind that you turned a key to start, not one that ran on 1929 technology and required you to take a bar to the flywheel to start, oil all the moving parts, and constantly monitor. I chewed on the inside of my lower lip, in the same way my mother does when she's nervous. I waited for Jeffrey to come back, hating that I didn't know much about how the engine works.

After a couple minutes, Jeffrey came up through the engine room scuttle. "Aaron's got to get a checklist. He forgot to open up the valve for the day tank and we almost ran out of fuel. He just won't fucking listen; thinks he can remember everything, and it turns out he can't. Look at him out there now, sound asleep."

I stared hard at Jeffrey. It wasn't like him to be so angry. He's usually very mellow. It wasn't really all that surprising, though; he was under a lot of stress.

"Don't be so hard on Aaron," I said hoping to calm Jeffrey down. "He's worked really hard the last two years, and this is a pretty big step for him. Remember how hard it was for you to run the engine when we first brought the boat to Bellingham?" I watched Jeffrey stare out the window. "If you recall, there was that one time when we came back to the dock and you forgot to do something and that caused the engine to speed up and run away on you. He'll figure it out soon."

"I know. There's just so much that can go wrong," Jeffrey replied. "Aaron's doing a fine job, but he still has so much to learn, and I don't want to be chief engineer *and* captain."

"I understand, but Aaron's still young and he's never been given this much responsibility before," I said, sensing that Jeffrey was returning to normal. "It will take some time, and you'll need to mentor him for a while. I'm sure that by the end of the season, he'll be a rock star when it comes to running the engine."

"Yeah, I know. I think I need to go wake him up and talk about what just happened." Jeffrey had returned to his normal demeanor and went out on deck.

I worried about all of our personalities and how well we would hold together. We would be on the boat and working in close quarters for a total of six weeks. I wondered what other trials we faced further down the road.

★

Later that afternoon, Sean was at the wheel while Jeffrey and Aaron talked on deck. I sat quietly hoping that everything at home would be all right. I already missed my cat, Harold, and wondered if he would miss me. I was happy that we had good house sitters who would be taking care of him.

What worried me more than the operation of the boat and the mental state of my cat was money. Our resources were exhausted, and Jeffrey had taken a large cash advance from one of our credit cards that he hoped would cover all of our bills. We had been bouncing checks like basketballs. It seemed that the moment we thought we had all of our bills paid, we'd forget about some automatic payment and be slapped with another round of overdraft fees. It felt as if we were drowning. I sighed, thinking how nice it was going to be to leave our financial disaster on shore for a few days. I couldn't wait to get into the wilderness and away from our checking account.

Money has always been my biggest obstacle, and I've often felt that I'm somehow a "money repellent." Any time cash gets too close to me, it gets deflected in another direction. I've spent a lot of time wondering how people with money make the opportunities that cause money to stick to them. It's one of those things that perplexes me. I know I've chosen a difficult path, trying to live a fulfilling lifestyle that's outside the mainstream, but I still believe the notion that if you work hard and have a passion, you'll be successful. When I think about our debt, I wonder about our chosen path and whether our hard work will lead us over a high cliff to our financial doom or if our path is just extra hilly and all this work will lead us to a successful and rewarding life.

The business of running a six-passenger boat is not an easy sell to investors or bankers. No one stands to make much money keeping an old wooden boat alive. Our desire to own and operate the *David B* is something we do for love and adventure, not for financial security and the hopes of an early retirement.

Unfortunately, it's hard to survive on love and adventure alone. Jeffrey's parents have been very supportive of the *David B* over the years, and the money that Aaron invested also went a long way, but it paled in comparison to what we really needed.

We bought the *David B* for $15,000. Jeremy said the engine was about the only thing of any value on the boat. At first we were able to pay for the projects we were doing with cash, but as we discovered more and more rot in the boat, the costs just kept climbing. We've mortgaged ourselves well into our next lives and have over $50,000 in credit card debt with ridiculously high interest rates, but we carry the burden of that debt proudly. We believe in ourselves and that running the *David B* is the right thing for us. "Go big or go home!" we joke to each other regularly.

Hopefully, we won't have to go home before we've made this business work. The specter of bankruptcy and losing everything we have striven for just adds to all the stress and uncertainty that comes with starting a new business. I'd rather live a life full of adventure but on the razor-thin edge of financial disaster than have a safe, dull life shoved inside a corporate box.

Years earlier, when I worked on a whale-watch boat, I talked with a woman who was unhappy with her job and her life. She wished for my summer job, but her desk job in a cubicle under a bank of florescent lights paid too well. Her words will always remain with me: "It's simply inhumane to place human beings inside windowless cubicles for eight hours a day."

Jeffrey returned to the pilothouse after discussing the importance of checklists with Aaron. We were getting close to Roche Harbor, and he needed to get the U.S. Customs paperwork in order. Unlike a pleasure craft, the *David B* is a commercial vessel, so we needed to let Customs know that we were going to Canada. Jeffrey couldn't find his Customs folder and had started tearing through his cabinets on the bridge deck.

"Are you sure it's not up here?" I asked, dreading that he was going to ask me to go below and face the mound of clothing, bedding, and tools that were piled sky-high in our unfinished cabin.

"I can't find it anywhere up here," he said. "I think I remember seeing the folder down by my side of the bunk. Can you go below and see if you can find it?" He gave me an urgent look.

"All right, I'll see what I can find." I reluctantly slid off my comfortable seat in the pilothouse.

I descended into the engine room. It was hot and smelled strongly of diesel. I stooped through the doorless break in the bulkhead that leads into our cabin, ignoring the pool of water on the floor. It was a mess. In our rush to finish the boat for passengers, we'd left our space in the very back of the boat undone. Its overall shape is a half-oval and ends at the rudder post. It has two bunks. The one we sleep on is tucked away on the port side of the boat. It's king-sized at the shoulders and tapers down to just enough space for our feet to snuggle together. The frames and the planking in this part of the boat are all new. I had barely had enough time to get them coated with a layer of gray primer paint before we moved aboard. The bulkhead that divides the engine room from our cabin is also unfinished, and it is really just a partially sectioned-off corner of the engine room. It gets hot during the day while the engine is running, with the temperature in the cabin regularly rising above ninety. I try not to be bothered by living in an unhealthy environment, since it is only for a few weeks. Even if I were bothered, there wasn't much that we could do about it until fall.

Once inside the cabin, I made a sharp right turn past the exhaust pipe, which comes over the top of the partially finished bulkhead. The pipe makes a ninety-degree bend above my side of the bunk before heading up into the pilothouse. Fiberglass from the wrapping on the exhaust sometimes flakes onto my pillow while the engine is running. There was enough light from the portholes to make a quick scan of the cabin. I didn't see the Customs folder, so I flipped on the light, shook off my clogs, and crawled up onto the bunk where our sea bags were stacked along with sleeping bags; extra blankets; a guitar, a violin, and a mandolin; as well as my spotting scope, cookbooks, a box of stuff I needed to file, and the bills that I would need to pay when we got to Ketchikan. After some digging, I found Jeffrey's folder and crawled back off the bunk.

As I backed down, I put my foot into the pool of water that I'd carefully ignored on my way in. It was cold, and I was annoyed that I would have to find a new pair of socks. Jeffrey was perplexed about where the water was coming from and why it only came in when we were underway. It was frustrating because we had just spent six months in the shipyard rebuilding the stern, and to have a leak was a big disappointment. The boat didn't leak when we were at anchor or tied to the dock. The only plausible explanation we could come up with was that water was pushed up through the wooden rudder post as the *David B* squatted down while it was underway. We were going to have to wait until next spring's haul-out to work on the leak. To fix the problem of having water on our floor, Jeffrey bought a couple bags of concrete and some plywood to reroute the water into the bilge, where it could be pumped out. A dry floor in our cabin would be nice, even if it was just hacked together.

I slid my shoes back on and stepped out of the cabin. I looked at my watch. It was late in the afternoon. We were almost to Roche Harbor and I'd need to think about dinner soon. As I passed though the doorway, I paused to watch the engine, its nine push-rods moving up and down to the beat of the three cylinders. We had a long way to go, but for the moment, things were all right.

CHAPTER 2

BIENVENUE AU CANADA

M/V David B -- Ship's Log					Date 6/19/2006
Time	Location	Wind	Baro	Depth	Remarks
0508	Anchored Roche Hrbr	NE	1030	18ft	Sky Clear
0730	UNDERWAY FROM ROCHE Hr				
0900	SECURE CUSTOMS DATA				

I FUMBLED WITH MY ALARM CLOCK. It was 0500.
From the porthole above our bed, cool air and early
morning light streamed down. I could see blue sky.
Good, I thought as I sat up and leaned over to kiss
Jeffrey. He still had a couple of hours to sleep, so I
quietly got dressed and left our cabin. I'm an
unapologetic morning person, and I relish being the
first up. It's a time of day when all things seem possible
and nothing is spoiled.

My first job of the morning is to make a log
entry. Outside, the sky was a soft pastel of light blue,
pink, and purple. It looked like it was going to be a
beautiful day. I flipped the page to a new day and
wrote down my observations:

TIME: 0508
WIND: NE at 3 knots
DEPTH: 18 feet
BAROMETER: 1030 millibars
SKY: Clear

Then I stepped down into the galley to start the stove. I store kindling and newspaper under the starboard-side seat cushion; I grabbed some of both to put into the firebox. On the left side of the stove are two nickel-coated half-spheres with handles sticking out. These bells, as they are called, control the airflow into the stove. I opened them up all the way. I've discovered that some newspapers burn better than others, with the maritime equivalent of the want ads, called *Boats and Harbors*, being the best fire starter, whereas *The Whatcom Watch* and *Bellingham Business Journal* both seem to be made of some sort of fire-retardant paper. I lit the fire and left the firebox door slightly open. While the fire starts, I plan my meals for the day.

Breakfast would be lemon-blueberry muffins, scrambled eggs, and a pork product, maybe bacon. For reasons that I don't understand, all the best breakfast meats seem to be made from pigs. I could make minestrone soup and fresh-baked bread for lunch, since the weather would be nice and the seas calm. If it had looked as if we would be in for rough weather, then something easy to eat, like sandwiches, would have been on the menu. We usually have breakfast and dinner at anchor, so I don't worry about those meals being weather-dependent.

With the fire going, I opened the pilothouse door to step on deck. The faint smell of wood smoke lingered in the still air outside. I heard the high, whistling call of a bald eagle that was perched atop a tall Douglas fir and the short, rapid breath of a harbor seal just a few feet off the boat. I brushed and braided my hair, cherishing this hushed window of time when I can coexist quietly with nature. Later in the day, these sounds will be drowned out by the hustle and bustle of people and the buzz of floatplanes landing and taking off in Roche Harbor. I've always felt that by eight a.m., the day is spoiled by the business of humans.

Back inside, I stoked the stove while I waited for the teakettle to boil. I like to have the first cup of coffee ready by six a.m. I keep two French presses on the stove for the strong black coffee that I often refer to as "starter fluid." I had almost a half hour to wait, so I pulled out the grinder and ground the beans in preparation for the crew's morning coffee rituals. Jeffrey, Sean, and I need our morning caffeine, or "medicine," to make the day right. Aaron doesn't drink coffee; he maintains that it's a dirty habit. The rest of us, however, are hopelessly hooked.

The muffins that were on the docket for the morning would take three bowls. In the largest bowl I added three cups of all-purpose flour, half a cup of sugar, half a cup of brown sugar, one-and-a-half teaspoons of baking powder, and a dash or so of salt. I gave the dry ingredients a swirl. I melted a stick and a half of butter on the stove. It had been a few minutes since I checked the firebox, so I twisted around, took a step to the left, and stuffed it with more wood, then swirled the butter. I stepped back to my counter but kept my ears tuned to the fire crackling and the water in the teakettle. In the second, smaller bowl, I added a cup of whole milk, two eggs, and the zest of a lemon. I lightly beat the ingredients together as I watched the sun begin to rise over the harbor and peek through the trees. I set the mixture aside. The thermometer on the stovetop read 550 degrees, meaning that the oven temperature was probably around 425. I grabbed my muffin tin from the top of the warming box and gave it a good spray of cooking oil before setting it on the counter. The pilothouse was starting to warm with the heat from the stove, and the light of the sun gave the space around me a warm glow. I stoked the fire and exhaled a relaxed breath. The teakettle began to simmer.

The last bowl was reserved for the muffin topping. I wanted to make enough topping to last a few days, so into this bowl I placed a cup of all-purpose flour in with a cup of brown sugar and a couple large handfuls of rolled oats. I again checked the firebox before grabbing a stick of butter out of the small fridge that's just opposite the stove. I used a cheese grater to grate about half of the cold butter, which I then mixed with my fingers into the dry ingredients. The rhythm of my thumbs moving against my fingertips carried me into a deep meditation. The grit of the sugar, the silk of the flour, and the bulk of the oats cleared all my thoughts until my fingers recognized that butter was spread evenly though the coarse mixture.

I walked out on deck to the freezer and returned with some blueberries, mixing one cup of them into the dry mixture until each berry had a light coating of flour. Next, I stirred in the liquids, filled the muffin tin with batter, sprinkled the muffins with topping, and slid them into the oven. I stoked the fire and added another stick of wood. The teakettle began to boil. It was time to make coffee.

After the coffee was brewed, I went back to the fridge and took out some bacon. The morning was marching on and it was nearing six o'clock. I took a cup of coffee to Jeffrey. He was still asleep, so I rubbed his shoulder and sang him an irritatingly happy good morning song and switched on the light.

"It's time to get up. I'm excited to get underway and through Canada Customs and Dodd Narrows today," I said as I kissed him on the cheek.

"What time again is slack water at Dodd?" Jeffrey asked in a groggy voice.

"Oh, I don't remember exactly, but I think it's sometime between twelve-thirty and thirteen-hundred. We should check again when you get up," I said.

I'd spent all winter planning our course to Alaska. Jeffrey had taught me how to use the current tables and how to figure the time of slack water for the narrows and tidal rapids that were like the gates of the Inside Passage. Our first, Dodd Narrows, dictated today's schedule.

Sean was up soon after the coffee was ready. He likes a little milk and sugar in his coffee and has his own special stainless steel cup with decorative rope work on the handle. Steam, lit up by the sun, escaped from the hole in his coffee cup's lid. He'd slept well, he said, sliding into the settee. His shaggy strawberry-blond hair was glowing a bit like a halo in the sunlight that illuminated the varnish in the pilothouse.

We had met Sean while he was the mate on the *Schooner Zodiac*. He's an excellent shipwright and sailor, and for the last year he had been an indispensable fixture on the *David B*. We knew we would need an extra hand taking the boat to Alaska because Jeffrey and Aaron would be spending a lot of time in the engine room working out the bugs with the engine. We asked Sean if he'd come along since he has a captain's license and could drive the boat without instruction. He agreed and was very excited about going to Alaska, especially about the day we planned to visit a tidewater glacier.

Sean took a slow sip of coffee as we chatted about what we hoped to see today. The smell of muffins just out of the oven drew Jeffrey up from our cabin.

"What's for breakfast?" was his first real sentence of the day.

"Lemon-blueberry muffins, eggs, and some bacon." I motioned to the table where I'd set out the muffins alongside some fruit I'd sliced up.

Jeffrey had his red bag of toiletries and his coffee mug with him. His mug was old, with a broken handle that had been epoxied back in place and a cartoon drawing of a crowd of Vikings. Bold capital lettering below the cartoon says the word NORGE. Jeffrey's never been to Norway, but it's his favorite mug and it goes with him everywhere. He handed me his NORGE mug and set his bag on the counter, then lay down on the floor to stretch his neck and lower back.

"Good morning, Captain," Sean said, watching Jeffrey's morning routine with interest.

"Good morning, Captain," Jeffrey joked as multiple vertebrae in his neck popped in an unsettling musical ascension.

After Jeffrey finished cracking his neck, he picked up the current tables to check on the time for slack water at Dodd Narrows.

"Looks like we need to have the anchor up at oh-seven to get to Dodd on time." Jeffrey confirmed what we already knew, but he was happy to double check just in case we'd missed some information in the current tables.

Aaron dragged himself into the pilothouse at 0645. He had just taken Havilah ashore and said his goodbyes to her. He was tired, and his humor wouldn't kick in until he had been awake for about an hour. Besides not liking coffee, Aaron doesn't eat breakfast, although if there is a pork product on the table he's likely to grab a sausage or slice of bacon on his way down to the engine room.

"Good morning," he grumbled and descended directly to start his engine.

With Aaron ready to go, Sean and Jeffrey broke from their conversation about what they were going to do when we got to Nanaimo. They both stood up and went out on deck to get ready to raise the anchor.

I stayed in the galley, wanting to wash a few dishes and make some bread. Aaron started the engine and adjusted the throttle before he climbed the scuttle and went out on deck, taking a slice of bacon with him.

"Hey, Christine," I heard Jeffrey call, "you should come up here and watch how we raise the anchor."

"All right," I said, putting aside the dirty dishes.

I left the galley and walked up to the bow. The guys were leaning over the lifelines, peering into the water as the windlass pulled up the chain. It was like a contest for them to see who could spot the anchor first. We had one shot, or ninety feet of chain, to pull up out of the water. It was attached to our 450-pound anchor. It was slow going, and my mind wandered back to when the *David B's* windlass was still sitting on the beach on Lopez Island. It probably weighs a thousand pounds, and at the time, I was sure that moving it from the beach to the boat would end in some kind of disaster.

When Jeremy first showed us the boat, Jeffrey had asked what happened to the windlass. Jeremy had sheepishly pointed to the beach where it was sitting.

"I was pulling on a mooring stone that was a little heavy, and I guess the deck was a bit soft. Then all of a sudden, the windlass went through the deck," Jeremy'd explained.

"Hmm. I bet that made a hell of a noise," Jeffrey had commented.

Jeremy had gone on to describe how he had craned the windlass onto the beach where it would remain while he planned to make repairs to the *David B's* deck.

I'd looked over to where Jeremy was pointing. The windlass's terrestrial position was aesthetically pleasing in the way that old discarded machinery often is, its faded green paint contrasted against the grey rock of the quarry and dried golden grasses left over from the previous summer. While I'd half-listened to Jeffrey and Jeremy talk about broken deck beams and planks, I'd wondered what the windlass looked like as it was pulled through the *David B's* foredeck and what it would take to get the windlass back onto the boat.

A year later, when we'd finished laying the new foredeck, it was time to move the windlass. Jeffrey had spent weeks thinking about this move and had come up with a plan.

"So, Jeremy knows a guy with a crane that we can hire to lift the windlass onto the boat," he'd told me one afternoon.

"He's not the guy with that crappy old crane in the parking lot, is he?" I asked.

"Yup," he replied, knowing that I wouldn't approve.

"And wasn't *that* crane somehow involved with the boat that got dropped over at the boat shed?" I asked with some suspicion, trying to see if Jeffrey was really thinking smart or if he was just worried about cost.

"I think he might have been involved, but I don't know for sure." Jeffrey smiled at me, knowing that I was uncomfortable with his plan. "Anyhow," he continued, "we can use his crane to lift the windlass off the beach and onto the boat. From what Jeremy said, he's not going to cost us much money. Some cash and a six-pack of beer should be enough."

"Hmm," I wondered, "do you really think this guy's going to be able to get the windlass onto the boat? That boom isn't anywhere near long enough." I pointed this fact out to Jeffrey, hoping to dash his sketchy plan. I was worried that we'd end up with the windlass in the water or Jeffrey somehow squished.

"Don't worry, it will be fine. This guy has been moving stuff with his crane for years." Jeffrey's confidence told me that his plan was safer than I imagined.

"Do I have to be there?" I asked.

"Well, since Michael will be here, I think we'll be fine without you," he said, then called me a chicken.

"That's good," I said with relief. "I think I'd bite a hole in my lower lip with worry if I had to be there."

Moving the windlass onto the boat was the last project we had to do to bring the *David B* to Bellingham. We were eager to get it on board, but there were many steps involved, and they all had to happen in the middle of a rising tide. The first was to pull the *David B* away from Jeremy's fleet of dying boats, which included not only the *Yakatat* but also an old ocean tug called the *David P Flemming*. Once the *David B* was free from its moorings, Jeffrey planned to haul her in close enough to the beach to let her bow ground out about twelve feet from the shore, up against the end of a set of decaying pilings that the crane operator had modified as a makeshift pier to drive his crane on. Instead of building a normal pier with crosswise planks, he had constructed his rickety pier by cutting two rows of old pilings to the same height and then laying a heavy plank lengthwise on each row, starting at the shore. This made two very skinny and unstable piers that were just wide enough for the crane's front tires.

The windlass move was scheduled for a weekday. It meant that Jeffrey couldn't change his mind at the last minute about me coming with him to be a part of this far-flung cowboy operation where injury or disaster seemed a given. I was happy that our friend Michael had flown here from Maine to help us with the last details of relocating the *David B* to Bellingham, including the windlass move.

Jeffrey wanted to get out to Lopez as early as possible on the day he was to have the windlass craned onto the *David B*, so Jeffrey and Michael left around five a.m. to catch the first ferry. I spent the day nervously pretending not to think about what danger they might be in near heavy things being lifted by half-broken equipment.

The crane, I knew, was vintage. I had studied its shape numerous times while working on the boat. It had two cabs; the cab in front was for driving the crane on the highway, but the crane's dilapidated appearance suggested that it had been a long time since it had seen the open road. It was about half the width of the vehicle, with just enough room inside for the driver to steer. The crane boom rested on what would have been the passenger side, and the engine was partially exposed behind the cab. The other, slightly larger cab for operating the crane was about twenty feet back. It was a dark blue and shaped like the gondolas in pictures of 1950s ski resorts. The windows in the crane cab had white frames that gave off the feeling of a cozy cottage, which was enhanced by the wildflowers that were growing up alongside the crane's wheels. The boom stuck out several feet from the truck. Its steel skeleton was black and rusty and about twenty or thirty feet long. Along with the crane cab, it could swivel in any direction. I imagined how Jeffrey and Michael were doing out on Lopez with the ancient crane and its eccentric operator. The day seemed to drag on, and I couldn't wait for the guys to come home safely.

When they did finally return to Bellingham, their eyes were red and they were wiping tears from their cheeks.

"What's going on? Is everything okay?" I asked with alarm. We didn't have cell phones back then, and

I'd been on pins and needles waiting for the car to pull into the driveway.

Jeffrey wiped his eyes. "It was hilarious!" he said, laughing.

Michael nodded in agreement with a big smile.

"It was so Lopez," Jeffrey said, referring to the Islanders' sort of "hack-and-go" approach to getting jobs done. "Instead of picking up the windlass, like a *normal* crane operator would, he just drug it across the gravel lot. When he spooled in the wire, it caused it to waddle like a penguin, tearing up everything in its path."

Michael rocked back and forth in place to demonstrate the motion of the windlass.

"It was like fucking R2D2, but with plants and rocks shooting out everywhere." Jeffrey laughed as Michael wobbled, whistling like a warbler. "We've been imitating it all day."

"But that's not the best part," Michael snorted.

"Oh yeah, the kicker. This is where the whole operation went totally Lopez." Jeffrey caught his breath and wiped his eyes. "So Michael and I were standing on the beach, ready for the crane guy to start up the crane and pick up the windlass, when he asks us to *unhook* the wire. 'What?' I said to him, and he again asked us to unhook the wire. So I undid the windlass. He then told us to take the wire out to a spot at the end of the pier and hook it up there because it turned out that while the motor for the boom worked fine, the engine to move the crane was busted and he had to pull the whole damn truck *around* with the winch."

"Oh my god, I'm so glad I wasn't there." I was astonished that I wasn't picking up one or both of them from the hospital.

"Wait, it gets better," Michael said.

"The pier had catastrophe written all over it, and getting the crane out onto it was sketchy." Jeffrey paused. "So, after Michael and I hooked up the wire to the end of the pier, the crane guy spooled in the wire. The truck inched out toward the narrow planks of the piers, and while the crane was spooling wire and inching forward, the crane guy got out with everything still running and scrambled up to the truck cab to steer out onto the pier. Once he was lined up, he'd run back to the crane cab to work the controls. He had to do this every time he needed to steer."

"Really?" I tried to imagine what the whole operation must have looked like.

"Yeah, and the best part was when he got out over the water and he couldn't go back and forth on the ground any longer. To stop, he had to climb out of the back cab and shinny out onto the chassis. Then, with the crane still moving, he balanced and scampered along the frame to the truck cab. At the last possible moment, he fell into the driver's seat and jammed on the brakes so he didn't roll off the pier and into the water."

"It was like a monster-sized inchworm heading for a slow-motion train wreck disaster. I've never seen anything like it," Michael said, trying not to bust up.

"He seriously winched the whole frigg'n crane out onto those planks. It was so sketch-ball," Jeffrey said. "You would have hated it."

"So how long did it take to get the windlass on the boat?" I asked.

"Oh, not long once the crane was out on the pier," Jeffrey said. "We hooked the wire around the windlass and then he picked it up. Michael and I guided it down into place and it was all done. Just like that. Now all we need to do is attach a new shaft and bolt it in." Jeffrey made his way to the fridge for a round of what we call "triumphant return beers." He handed Michael and me each a beer.

Michael took his beer, rocked side to side, and made a couple more R2D2 whistles—causing another round of giggles out of the two of them.

"The flukes are out of the water," Sean said to Aaron, who was ready at the clutch to stop the windlass from hauling up any more chain. I leaned over the lifelines to get a better look at the anchor out of the water.

"Okay. Three, two, one, stop," Sean said as the anchor slid into place.

Aaron clutched out the windlass and put the brake on before going down to the engine room. I smiled, remembering the whole ordeal of the crane and getting the windlass on to the *David B*. It seemed like another lifetime when Michael and Jeffrey were out on Lopez with the mostly broken crane.

I can't believe we're here on the second day of the journey we had been preparing for, for so long.

I turned to watch Jeffrey shift the *David B* into ahead as I walked down the starboard side of the boat and into the galley. The engine's waltz sped up and we were underway for Canadian waters.

It didn't take long for us to cruise past Spieden and Stuart Islands and cross the border into Canada. The Customs dock was in Bedwell Harbour on South Pender Island, and checking in was delightful since we didn't have any passengers on board. Jeffrey gathered up our passports and walked up to the phone that automatically dials the Customs office.

"What did they say about the wine?" I asked when Jeffrey returned from the phone booth.

"*Bienvenue au Canada.* No problem with the wine. We just can't drink any of it while we're in Canada. If we do and they catch us, they'll make us pay 150 percent tax on the total amount of wine, so just don't break any," he said.

"I don't think that will be a problem. They are all secure in the starboard cabin," I said as Jeffrey handed back our passports.

The wine was for the Australians, our first real paying passengers, and they were the reason we were heading to Alaska. They had informed us that they didn't drink beer and asked me to upgrade the wine I planned to serve on board. With the help of one of the wine shops in town, I put together a mix of seventy-two bottles of wine for their eight-day trip. I hoped the mostly Washington wines I had bought would be good enough and would pair well with the menu I had planned for them. I had three weeks to wait to find out, so I put it out of my mind and just felt relieved that we were in Canada and had made it through Customs without any kind of hassle.

Once we were underway again, we had about five hours to get to Dodd Narrows in time for slack water. Jeffrey kept checking his watch and the speed of the *David B* to make sure we were going to make it.

While we cruised, Jeffrey explained how the tides and currents worked to make the tidal rapids that we were to encounter on the first few of days of our journey and why it was so important that we arrive at Dodd Narrows at the right time.

"So, the water from the Pacific Ocean meets up with Vancouver Island and has to go around it from either the North or South." Jeffrey grabbed a pen and searched for some paper. Not finding any, he started what has proven to be a bad habit: sketching in the logbook and drawing directly over the entries. "The water flows in from the south through the Strait of Juan De Fuca while water from the north streams down Johnstone Strait and Queen Charlotte Strait."

I leaned over to look at Jeffrey's drawing of Vancouver Island and the other islands he'd quickly drawn. The straits extended to where I'd earlier written the morning's barometer reading.

"Are you still with me?" he asked.

"Yeah, what's odd is that most of the rapids are along the central part of Vancouver Island," I said. "I guess that's because there are so many islands that are close to each other."

"Yeah, so, as the tides come and go, the water gets restricted between a few narrow spots." Jeffrey scribbled many arrows all coming together. "It's in these bottlenecks that the tidal rapids form as tremendous amounts of water push through these passages. In places such as Skoocumchuck Rapids, the water can race along at sixteen knots."

"Right, and in our daily twice-high and twice-low cycle of tides, there are two times each day where the water in these passages goes slack for a few minutes and we can easily pass," I contributed, to let Jeffrey know that I was paying attention.

As we neared Dodd Narrows, boats started to appear as if out of nowhere and the VHF radio came to life with security calls warning of boaters entering the channel. It was like being in a parade. Jeffrey steered the *David B* into our place in the lineup for the slack water.

"Hey guys, you'll want to get your cameras out. This is going to be fun." Jeffrey turned to Sean and me and handed me my camera. "Hey, Aaron," Jeffrey said next, "can you go slow us down just a bit?"

Before going out on deck, I watched Jeffrey as he methodically kept an eye out for oncoming traffic and monitored our position on the chart plotter to make sure we were in the right spot. The entrance to Dodd Narrows has on one side a steep rocky cliff and on the other a low shoreline that gives way to a small grassy patch with a bench for spectators. We entered only a few feet off the shoreline. I felt as if we were close enough to the beach that we could have leaned over the lifelines to shake hands with the folks on shore.

When we entered Dodd Narrows, we were in the posh Southern Gulf Islands, and in the minute or so it took to cruise through the Narrows, we passed into the outskirts of the natural-resource-based working-class town of Nanaimo.

Directly in front of us as we exited Dodd Narrows was a log dump where hundreds of logs were corralled alongside a series of pilings. Workers were in the process of tying the logs together with thick wire cables to make a huge raft that could be towed to some unknown destination.

"Log bronc, log bronc, log bronc!" Jeffrey shouted out and pointed to the log dump with the kind of excitement that a birder might exhibit upon seeing a spotted owl.

I was still up on deck while Jeffrey was jumping with excitement.

"Nice spot," I teased Jeffrey with my birder's lingo. "What does a log bronc do? It's super cute, like a Little Toot." I said, girlishly mocking the little tough-guy boat.

"Yes, Christine, they are cute. You're right about that, but they are total work horses. Check that one out," Jeffrey said as I walked back to the pilothouse to take the binoculars he was holding out the window.

The log bronc looked like a stubby tugboat. It was about twenty feet long and had a standing-room-only pilothouse. It was highly maneuverable and bobbed a lot in the water. The man on the log bronc was working his boat like a marine cowboy rustling up a wild herd of logs.

Ever since we bought the *David B*, I had begun to develop a taste for workboats and for the work that each kind of boat does. I have been awed at the number and kind of boats that work in plain sight and yet relative obscurity. I've lived my whole life in the Pacific Northwest and somehow I had never noticed these boats before. The log broncs, like the *David B* when it was built, serve a specific purpose, and it's in that purpose that I find respect for them and the people who run them. While a big, shiny white mega-yacht might catch my eye for a moment, it's the boats like the log broncs, old tugs, and fishing boats that really draw my interest.

After the excitement of learning about log broncs, Jeffrey asked me to find out on which channel to call the Port of Nanaimo's harbormaster.

"It says here you can call the harbormaster on channel six-seven," I said, letting him know after flipping to the page on Nanaimo's harbor in the guidebook. "It's such a hassle to have to stop in Nanaimo to finish provisioning. I wish we didn't have to stop to get, beer, wine, and potatoes."

"Yeah, well, thanks to the government of Canada, we're only allowed to bring two bottles of wine, 750 milliliters of spirits or 24 cans of beer, and no fruit and/or vegetables with a pit, a core, or an eye into the country." Jeffrey rattled off a version of the speech he had given more than 500 times to passengers going to Canada, when he worked as captain on the *Victoria Star*.

After acknowledging my irritation, Jeffrey turned around and unhooked the microphone of the marine radio, then dialed channel 67 and called the harbormaster, who assigned us a spot on the inside of the breakwater.

"Hey, Sean, can you look through the binoculars and tell me what our place on the dock looks like?" Jeffrey asked.

"Roger," Sean answered and scanned the dock. "So, it looks like there are two pretty big white yachts you're going to have to parallel park between, Captain."

"Roger that," Jeffrey said slowly, then asked Sean, "Do you think you could have a quick look at what the tide is doing?"

Sean opened the tides program on the computer and said, "The tide is flooding, so I think you're going to be set off the dock while we're tying up."

"Roger that," Jeffrey said again as he sized up our situation.

It made my stomach turn, thinking that Jeffrey was going to have to parallel park between two gleaming white multimillion-dollar boats. Even though I trusted Jeffrey's ability and knew how much he loved docking, this sort of maneuvering between expensive yachts made me nervous. The *David B*, unlike the boats that we were to settle in between, doesn't have any bow thrusters—which Jeffrey considers cheating—and therefore docking the *David B* requires a lot more skill and forethought than it takes to drive most modern yachts.

While Jeffrey jockeyed the boat into position, the sound of the engine caught the attention of people on the pier so that soon a crowd began to gather to watch Jeffrey squeeze the *David B* into our assigned spot. Jeffrey piloted the *David B* just past one of the boats and put her into reverse, then began to "walk" the boat closer to the dock. It was difficult, and the current was doing everything it could to keep us off. I stood on the starboard side of the boat with my fender ready and watched the long strands of seaweed from under the dock waving in the strong current. I hoped Jeffrey had more confidence in what we were doing than I did. We were getting closer, but we were still too far from the dock for Sean to make a leap. I listened to the whooshing of air from the shifter as Jeffrey moved the *David B* a little more forward, then a little more backward as he fought against the current. Jeffrey, Sean, Aaron, and I were all keeping an eye on the distance between us and the two boats on either end of the *David B*. Our progress was painfully slow: three feet, then two feet, then Jeffrey would shift into ahead and the *David B* would gain momentum and we'd pull away from one of the pricey yachts and inch closer to the other while he steered the boat so that we were inching sideways.

I could tell that people on the boats on either side of us were not very comfortable with us and our old boat and engine. This was especially true of a couple of disapproving older women dressed in their finest yachting clothes. Their navy-blue shirts were festooned with white and gold ribbons. One had golden stars on her shoulders and the other a golden ship's wheel embroidered across her chest. I figured their unease and disapproving looks had a lot to do with their husbands' abilities to bring in their own boats.

Among the nervous women and a few amused men was an older gentleman. He was dressed in a very yacht-y manner with a smart dark blue sports blazer, a white pressed shirt, and Greek fisherman's cap. From my position I couldn't see his shoes, but I guessed they had white soles and dark leather uppers. He stood, bent at the waist and leaning on his boat's railing. His slightly angled arms were spread apart, and his large hands gripped the wide teak rail. The size and roughness of his hands suggested that he had not always lived a life of luxury. He watched us very closely, but not with the same nervousness as the others around him. He had a different expression. The sound of the engine appeared to be music to his ears, and if he had any concern for Jeffrey's ability to get the *David B* to the dock without crashing into his boat, it didn't show. The one-two-three waltz of the Washington Iron Works engine sang out its siren song to him. He tapped his right index finger to the rhythm.

Sean's moment to get to the dock came, and he leapt gracefully off the *David B* with the spring line in hand. With lightning speed, he made a couple of wraps around the bull rail and shouted back to Jeffrey, "Spring's on!"

Jeffrey looked out the window and gave the boat a little power, which sucked the *David B* securely into the dock. With the engine still in gear, Aaron and I stepped off and joined Sean in tying up the boat while politely answering questions for three or four people who remained gathered on the dock. When we had finished with the lines, Jeffrey came out on deck, checked that the boat was tied up the way he wanted, and then took the boat out of gear. "Finished with engines," he said to Aaron, who went below to shut it down.

"No bow thruster, eh?" The gentleman on the boat behind us with the blazer and fishermen's cap spoke out to Jeffrey.

"Nope," Jeffrey said with a hint of pride.

"Very nice job. What's she powered with? A Gardner?" the gentleman asked.

"No, not a Gardner, a Washington. I think they must have sounded similar. Lots of people ask if we have a Gardner," Jeffrey answered.

The gentleman took a long look at the boat, then spoke again. "What was she used for?"

"She was built to beat a fishing regulation in Bristol Bay, Alaska. At the time the regulations said that all fishing was to be done under sail. Power was not allowed. The lawyers for the canneries took a long look at the regs and found a loophole. Nowhere did it say that you couldn't tow a bunch of boats to the fishing grounds. So this boat, which they called a Monkey Boat, was built to take string of the 32-foot-long sailboats out to fishing grounds from the cannery. We still have the towing bit." Jeffrey moved aside and pointed to the large ironbark bit on our back deck.

"What year was she built?" he asked.

"Nineteen twenty-nine, at Lake Washington Shipyards just outside of Seattle, in what is now Kirkland."

"How long was she in Alaska?" He leaned further over his boat's railing.

"She worked from 1929 until 1951, when the rules changed. Once they could fish under power, the *David B* became obsolete, and they pulled her up on the beach on a cradle and she sat there until 1981, when a woman who fishes up there brought the boat back to Seattle."

"Very interesting. She sure is a nice-looking boat. Did you do the work, eh?" he asked.

"Sure did." Jeffrey beamed.

"That's an awful lot of work," the gentleman said with a smile suggesting that he knew something about wood boats and how much care they take. "Who was she built for?"

"The company that had the boat built was Libby, McNeill, Libby," Jeffrey explained. "They still make Vienna sausages and potted meat. But back in that day they had a huge operation in Alaska, canning salmon."

"Well, she's a nice boat to look at. Good on you for keeping her going." The gentleman straightened up and smiled.

In 1999, a year or so after we bought the boat, Jeffrey was looking around online for some information about the *David B*. We knew that the boat was named after one of Libby's cannery managers, but we didn't know for sure what his last name was. Jeremy had told us it was maybe Brach or Branch.

"Hey, check this out," Jeffrey said, leaning back in his computer chair.

"Yeah, what did you find?" I leaned over in my chair to look at the screen.

"A boat with the name *David W. Branch*. It was once owned by Libby. Do you think it could be named after the same guy as our *David B*?" Jeffrey gave me a look of hope that he'd found a key piece of the puzzle of the *David B's* history.

"I don't know. Maybe it's the same guy. It sure would be nice to know. Did you try typing in that full name?" I leaned in closer to the computer screen to try to get a better look at the image of the large ship.

"Not yet. Let me see what I can come up with." Jeffrey typed out the name slowly, like a shaman calling out to the ancestors. His pinky finger hovered over the return key for just a second, as if apprehensive about what the answer w   reveal. I leaned in close to him as he pressed the   The computer thought for a moment or two and   applied the answer: nothing. We both sat back, disappointed. Then Jeffrey scrolled down a bit.

"Hey, wait. Look at this," Jeffrey said, reading the results. "David W. Branch, DDS, and he's in Seattle. Maybe it's his son."

"Well, click on it," I said, trying to get Jeffrey to move along a little faster. This was exciting. The result was a website for a dentist. We looked at the pictures and wondered if this David Branch was somehow related to our *David B*. Jeffrey clicked onto the Contact Us page, and we sat looking at a phone number and an e-mail address.

"What do we do?" Jeffrey turned his gaze from the screen to me.

"I don't know. I'm kind of scared. It's a bit like looking for your birth mother. What if you find her and she turns out to be a dud?" I said, thinking about a friend who was adopted and had recently had that experience.

"I think e-mail would be the best. That way, if he's related, he can respond back to us if he feels like it," Jeffrey said.

He leaned forward and clicked on the e-mail link. The screen popped up and Jeffrey began to write. "What do I say?"

"How about 'Hi, my name's Jeffrey Smith, and I have an old boat named *David B* that I think is named after your father. Are you related to someone with that name who worked for Libby, McNeill, Libby? If so I'd like to know about him. Here's my contact info,'" I said, without too much thought.

Jeffrey wrote something and then pressed send. "I wonder what we'll learn?"

The next day there was a reply in Jeffrey's inbox from David Branch. Jeffrey read through it a couple times.

"What did he say?" I asked impatiently.

"He's not David Branch's son," Jeffrey said. "He's his grandson! Check it out. He sent a newspaper clipping with a picture from his grandfather's retirement announcement. It says 'David Branch—A Friend to All Alaska.'"

"Let me see." I moved my chair over next to Jeffrey as he began to read the article aloud. It was interesting to read the description of who David B was, but more intriguing was the picture of the man the boat was named after. He had dark hair and a handsome face. David Branch's grandson had known about the *David W Branch* and that it had been used as a troopship in World War II, but he didn't know that our *David B* existed.

I stared at the face of the person whose namesake had so deeply changed my life. The connection to that face and name, and that person's life from so many years ago, made the *David B* seem more complete. It reminded me again of my friend who had recently found her birth mother. She often complained that she didn't have an origin story, and that emptiness was what drove her curiosity to find her birth mother. Looking at David Branch's picture felt a little like finding the boat's birth father. His picture and the brief story about his working life gave our *David B* its origin story.

"So," Jeffrey said, startling me back into the present as I sat enjoying the afternoon sun in Nanaimo. "Do you need any help with the groceries?"

"No, I'll be all right on my own. The grocery store and the liquor store are just a block or so from here," I replied.

"Great," Jeffrey said. "Sean, do you want to come with me to the chart store? How about you, Aaron? What's on your schedule?"

"Sure," Sean answered.

"Uh, nothing," Aaron said.

"Good. Aaron, you should come to the chart store with me and Sean. I don't think you'll want to miss out." Jeffrey smiled.

It was late afternoon when I was done with buying groceries. Luckily, the liquor store was right next door to the grocery, and I planned a quick stop for beer and wine. I pushed the cart out of the grocery and over to the liquor store, but as I lined the cart up to go through the automatic doors, the door didn't open. I stopped, looked through the glass doors. It was oddly dark. I tried the door again. Then I looked over to the store's hours to discover that the store was closed and had been since five o'clock. *What the fuck? What kind of backward-ass place that only allows you to bring two bottles*

of wine into the country would close its damn liquor store so damn early in the evening, on a Monday, no less? Five p.m. That's ridiculous. I yanked the cart back and started across the parking lot, disappointed that we were going to have to wait until nine tomorrow morning to buy beer and wine and that we wouldn't be getting an early start as Jeffrey had hoped.

Back on board, I unloaded all my apples, potatoes, and peaches, noting with a bit of irritation that the apples were imported from the United States and had been grown in Washington State.

"Hey Christine," I heard Jeffrey say as he stepped over the bulwarks, about a half hour after I got back. "You should have come to the chart store with us. The guy who runs the place sure is something else."

"He's like a Catholic priest or something," Aaron said.

"Yeah, and I don't think he's ever been on a boat, but he seems to know everything about every chart and every place on each chart," Jeffrey went on. "Oh, and Christine, you'll like this. The Chart Reverend thinks we should go through Venn Passage up by Prince Rupert. It will cut off eighteen miles on our last day between Prince Rupert and Ketchikan.

"Really? Venn Passage sounds kind of scary. Everything I've read about it says that the buoys don't stay put. There's a ton of range boards to line up on, and there are shallows everywhere." I knew how much Jeffrey loves that kind of navigation.

"Aw, come on, Christine. It'll be fun," Jeffrey teased me.

"Well, all right. I guess if the Holy Chart Reverend says it's okay, then we can go there," I said, thinking that Venn Passage was still ten days away so I would have plenty of time to warm up to the idea. Besides I was more interested in Jeffrey's eight hundred dollars' worth of new charts, and I wanted to paw though them.

Although we mostly relied on a computerized chart program that runs off GPS, Jeffrey didn't want to depend on the computer alone. If the electronics failed, we now had all the charts.

"So, guys, it sounds like you all had a fun field trip, but I have some bad news." I paused. "The liquor store was closed."

"What?" Aaron said first, fastest, and loudest. "What kind of dumb-ass country would close its liquor store on a Monday afternoon?"

"Canada, evidently," Sean said.

"So, what are our options? Is there a non-government store somewhere we could walk to or take a taxi?" Aaron was alarmed that we might leave Nanaimo without beer.

"I looked through the Nanaimo visitors guide and couldn't find one," I said. "I'm sure there is one here somewhere, but I just don't know where. The liquor store I went to opens at nine a.m. tomorrow."

"This is bullshit. We can't leave until the liquor store opens after nine in the morning? Canada's fucked," Aaron said.

"Well, that's going to be a little later than I wanted to leave." Jeffrey shrugged. "We've got to get to Desolation Sound tomorrow to stay on track, and I think it's going to take us ten or eleven hours from here, depending on if we can cross through the Whiskey Golf Military Zone," Jeffrey said trying to figure out how to handle this new emergency. He didn't want to leave Nanaimo without beer, either, since we all really liked an end-of-the-day, anchor-is-down beer.

After a few anxious moments, Jeffrey decided that if we were forced to stay in Nanaimo until the liquor store opened up, we might as well top off the fuel tanks in the morning. Staying in Nanaimo a little longer would also give Jeffrey and me some time to go for a run the next morning.

"Got your fast shoes ready?" Jeffrey asked in the dark of our cabin while I dug through my clothes to find my running shorts and a shirt.

"Yup," I replied. "How long do you want to go for?"

"I don't know. How does forty-five minutes sound to you?" Jeffrey sat up in bed, waiting for me to get dressed so he could use the small space with standing headroom in our cabin.

"That sounds perfect. I've never explored Nanaimo. Did you see it looked like there was a trail that runs along the waterfront? Do you want to start there?"

"Yeah, I was thinking the same thing."

"Great. I'll go start the stove and heat up some water for coffee while you get ready."

We stepped onto the dock. Nanaimo had a groggy feeling to it in the stillness of the morning. The sky was clear, and the air felt cool and a bit damp. We simultaneously lifted our wrists to start the timers on our watches as we took our first steps. As we left the dock and explored the waterfront, we chatted about our successes and our hopes in running the *David B.*

The streets were empty, except for a garbage truck backing up somewhere in the distance. Its reverse warning beeped out a wake-up alarm to the sleepy city. On our run through Nanaimo, it seemed that only the homeless and other runners pounded the pavement in the early morning.

For me, running is a sacred time to spend with Jeffrey. We focus, plan, and sort out our problems together when we run. At home, we run for hours on the forest trails that wind their way through the Chuckanut Mountains. The soft ground of the single-track trails is kind to our knees, while the tall trees shade us from the hot summer sun and shelter us from the cold rains of winter.

Most days when we run, we hit the trail with a problem to solve or a new idea. With each step we take up steep hills or through dense forest, my mind clears. We both become energized with possibilities while pileated woodpeckers knock on Douglas fir trees and ravens call with their deep-throaty "kwoak." The leaves and branches that gently reach out to brush against my arms and legs feel like a careful caress that lets me know that everything will be all right. While my eyes take in the bright green mosses, sword ferns, and rocks sticking out of the dark soil, we talk about fasteners, plumbing, decking, electrical wiring, and far-off anchorages in Alaska. It's here, amongst the trees on the steep, root-covered trails, that Jeffrey and I release our bodies from the crushing stress of rebuilding an old boat, starting a business, and running out of money.

The trails in the hills around Bellingham are the foundation of our marriage and our love. We bind ourselves together with the questions we ask one another and the mud that splashes up around our feet and onto our legs. The forest is our cathedral where we ask for answers. The silence of our thoughts as we push ourselves up slick rain-washed trails is where our answers come from. When the silence is broken by the fast chatter of a winter wren, we talk some more, and before the end of another run, we come to conclusions. Every aspect of our lives together is resolved while we are running, as the trees listen in silence.

Our run in Nanaimo was pleasant; we explored the city for an hour, not really going anywhere. Jeffrey was worried about the alternators and why they kept chirping. Not knowing much about how the alternators worked, I listened as Jeffrey talked his way through the *David B's* entire electrical system and racked his mind for the answer that still eluded him upon our return to the boat.

CHAPTER 3

A BMW WITH TWO 16-FOOT PLANKS

M/V David B -- Ship's Log					Date 26 June 2006

Time	Location	Wind	Baro	Depth	Remarks
0615	Docked - Nanaimo	Ø	1028	~	Clear
1230	UNDERWAY FROM NANAIMO				TOOK ON 150 gal DIESEL
2310	ANCHORED GALLEY	RAIN		LTNG	72 ....

WE WERE OFF THE DOCK around twelve-thirty with enough fuel, beer, and wine to make it to Ketchikan. The stretch between Nanaimo and Desolation Sound is long, and we planned to anchor sometime after dark.

We'd been underway for less than an hour when Jeffrey radioed Winchelsea Island Control to make sure that the Canadian Armed Forces were not going to be busy shooting off live torpedoes in a large area of the Strait of Georgia that's referred to as "Whiskey Golf." I looked up at the chart as Jeffrey waited for Winchelsea Control to answer. Whiskey Golf is simply marked on the chart as "WG" in large grey letters, and a large grey rectangular line outlines the area. Red lettering below the "WG" states "see WARNING/Voir AVERTISSEMENT. Armed Forces equipment tests are frequently conducted in Exercise Area WG as defined in Notice to Mariners No 35 of each year . . ."

✫

59

They claim that boats straying into Whiskey Golf will be fired upon if they do not leave immediately when the area is active. The voice from Winchelsea Control radioed back to Jeffrey that Whiskey Golf was inactive and that we were clear to transit through the area.

My big project for the day was to give birth to a sourdough starter. As part of my preparation for running the *David B*, I had taken a sixteen-week-long intensive culinary course in pastry. By the time I had finished the course, I had seriously fallen in love with baking bread and wanted to have my own sourdough starter to be able to bake rich and flavorful breads. My course instructor suggested I pick up a copy of Nancy Silverton's *Breads from the LaBrea Bakery* for a recipe for making a starter. I had everything with me and I was ready to go. I read the chapter on making the starter two or three times, just to make sure I knew exactly what I was doing.

As we motored across the Strait of Georgia and through the quiet Whiskey Golf Military Zone, I meticulously mixed together flour and water. Next, I swaddled a bunch of red seedless grapes in cheesecloth. I held the grapes over the container and squished them gently so that their juices flowed between my lightly floured fingers. I mixed the grape juice into the flour and water and then set the cheesecloth with the grapes into the mixture. The skins of the grapes were home to the natural yeasts that would live and die over countless generations in the pasty glop. The flour was going to provide food for the yeasts, and the water was the medium in which my new charge was to grow, develop, and mature.

For the next two weeks, I was committed to changing out a cup or two of flour and water each day to care for and love my newly born sourdough. I placed the lid on the container and gave it a small love pat to welcome it into the world.

I popped up on to the bridge deck after I had cleaned up my mess in the galley. "Guess what I just did? I just made a sourdough starter. I can't wait to see what it does over the next couple of weeks. I wonder if it will get all gross and bubbly?" I was really excited to nurture my new pet project.

My desire for a sourdough starter was also for the day I might forget to buy yeast. Having a sourdough starter was an insurance policy of sorts to make sure that we could always have fresh bread on board.

"Does it have a name?" Jeffrey asked.

"Oh, yes it does." I'd been thinking about its name while I stirred its ingredients together. "Its name is 'Whiskey Golf.'" I paused. "I was also thinking that W.G. should be its nickname, and that W.G. qualifies for dual citizenship since it was born in Canadian waters on an American boat."

"Uh, roger that," Jeffrey said. "You think you're pretty funny, don't you?"

"Oh yes, I am funny, but that's only because I'm tired," I jumped up onto one of the pilothouse seats to settle down for a while as we crossed Whiskey Golf.

I watched the surface of the water for porpoises and sea lions. Jeffrey started talking about how far we had come over the last few years.

"I'm so happy, Christine. I can't believe we're actually doing this. We are heading to Alaska in our own boat that we rebuilt ourselves. I was just thinking about how much your family helped in the rebuild. Remember when your parents came to help us move the wood from Jeremy's shop?"

"Oh, yeah, when Dad brought his convertible BMW to move planks around?" I said.

"Yeah, that time." Jeffrey laughed.

"You know, if I'd been paying closer attention to the car that day, I should have been suspicious when my parents drove up."

"How so?" Jeffrey asked.

"Well, Dad had a hardtop on the car, and if I remember right, it was an amazingly beautiful sunny day. A convertible kind of day. He would never have driven all the way up I-5 with the hardtop unless he'd had a plan." I had just put this together for the first time: my dad had spent a fair amount of time scheming about the best way to help us transport some long and heavy planks of wood.

When my mom, dad, and uncle arrived to help that Saturday, Jeffrey and I were already working. Our goal for the weekend was the beam shelf. It was one of the first new pieces of wood we were going to be putting into the boat after many weekends of removing the tar-soaked plywood and rotten decking that made up the foredeck. We were trying not to be discouraged by the amount of rot we were running into. Nothing could be saved. What had been the foredeck now sat in a heap at the base of the rock quarry, waiting to be burned.

"They're here," I said to Jeffrey when I spotted the white convertible in the parking lot. Jeffrey set down his notebook, and we walked across the swing float to my parents' car. The air was still and had the fresh smell of warm fir trees and ripening blackberries. It was going to be a prefect day to get stuff done.

"Good morning! Glad to see you both," Steve, my dad, said, adjusting his sweatshirt and jeans as he stepped out of the car. He was ready for work.

"How was the ferry ride?" I asked.

"Your father had two Portside sandwiches," my Uncle Rick snickered into my ear as he stepped out of the car. It was Rick's first trip to see the boat he'd helped Jeffrey and me purchase. He tugged on his mustache as he walked over to the water's edge to get a better look at the *David B.*

"I guess that means it was a good trip," I replied and turned to my mom, who agreed the ferry ride had been fun for all and that, yes, my dad had overindulged in Portside breakfast sandwiches.

Jeffrey was anxious to get started. We weren't going to be getting anything done just standing around in the parking lot, and even though it was only nine or so in the morning, the day felt like it was already half over.

"Okay guys, today's project is to take these planks of wood over to Jeremy's shop, where we'll plane them down to the right thickness. Once were done over there, we'll bring the planks back here so we can shape them into the beam shelf."

We had a large stack of beautiful old-growth clear Douglas fir planks we had bought for the foredeck project. The planks were big and heavy—measuring four inches thick, fourteen inches wide, and sixteen feet long—and sat covered under a brown tarp. Jeremy had suggested that we use only brown tarps, since the blue ones were unsightly.

I struggled with my values and the stack of wood. I was willingly buying wood from trees that I felt were sacred. I made justifications to myself for the use of old-growth timber. In my mind I told myself that our project was noble and that the trees would be happy to sacrifice their lives for the time-honored craft of wooden boat building.

The reason for buying old growth is the tightness of the wood's grain. When a tree grows in a forest for hundreds of years, it grows slowly, stretching itself toward the canopy and reaching for sunlight. When you cut it down and look at the rings, they are close together, sometimes so close it's hard to count. Each ring marks a year in the tree's life, and the slow growth of a tree in a natural forest produces very tight rings. It's the closeness of the grain that gives wood its strength, beauty, and resistance to rot. When I work with old-growth wood, I give thanks to the tree that gave its life and to the animals who lost their homes and their habitat.

Before the family had arrived, Jeffrey and I made a series of measurements in the gaping hole where the foredeck had recently been. We had removed some of the bunks, but there were still piles of engine parts, a fifty-five-gallon drum, and a potbelly stove to work around. The entire foredeck was gone, along with the beams that the decking sat on and the shelf that the beams rested upon. There was a lingering smell of tar and bark mulch that was specific to the *David B's* geriatric condition.

We propped ourselves up against the ceiling planking. Jeffrey handed me the bevel gauge. It was a simple tool, folded in half, about six inches long, with a wing nut at the pivot. The black handle had a slit inside which a thin, flat, shiny blade of metal was nestled. It was another new tool to me. I was in a crash course in wooden boat restoration, and the tools were being presented to me in rapid fire. I was curious about what we were going to be doing with this one.

I feared some math might be coming my way, but as much as I was afraid, I knew it was good for me. My third-grade teacher once told the student sitting next to me, "Don't ever cheat off Christine. She'll never get the right answer." For me, math in books is mostly impossible. I just can't wrap my brain around the concepts as they are presented in a text. Since buying the *David B* and having been forced to solve real problems, however, I had begun to realize that I really did understand more about it than I thought.

Jeffrey, who excels in math, would explain formulas to me that I needed to help me solve some math-related problem on the boat. Since it was a real physical problem, the math was so much easier. I wished I'd had an old wooden boat to learn math on in elementary school.

Jeffrey opened the bevel gauge. "This tool is for transferring angle measurements. You'll want to make a measurement every foot or so until you get to the bow. It's easy." He smiled. "Then take the gauge, place it on this piece of scrap plywood, and trace down the inside. That's your bevel board. It will show us the angles that I'll need to shape the backside of the beam shelf. Don't forget to mark the spots where you measured onto the ceiling planking."

I took the bevel and remembered all the humiliation I'd felt in school when I was called to the chalkboard to solve some problem. I would just stand there, paralyzed, staring at the chalkboard. Holding onto the bevel, I thought about how I had to take Algebra 101 twice in college and how I had just barely gotten a D in geometry in high school. My degree is in anthropology because the math requirements were minimal. This real-world math was challenging, yet Jeffrey made it seem simple. I knew I needed to be exact for the piece to fit, and despite the weight of a lifetime of mathematical failure sitting on my shoulders, I knew I could do this.

Now that my family was here, it was time to get to work. "Hey, Steve, Rick; can you guys give me a hand with this tarp?" Jeffrey asked.

"Sure," they said in unison.

I lingered with my mom for a few moments to catch up and talk about wedding details. Jeffrey had asked me to marry him several months ago. We were committed to each other and to a future together with this boat.

"We think we found a place," I announced, unable to get eye contact with Mom as she kept a wary eye on Dad. I could tell by the way she was biting down on her lip that she was nervous about something.

"Where?" she asked, carefully watching my dad.

"In La Conner, on the water, at a place with beautiful gardens. We can have the wedding either inside or outside if the weather cooperates," I said, wondering why Mom was so preoccupied with my dad.

"That'll be nice. What's it like?" she answered, trying to pay attention to me.

"It's really pretty. The décor is art deco, and outside there is a wrought-iron gazebo that juts out over the water. I think it will be perfect."

"Sounds nice," she said, then turned to watch my dad. "I'm worried your father won't do what Jeffrey wants."

"I think Dad will do fine. Besides, what could possibly go wrong?" I smiled.

"You know your father. He's liable to do just about anything." She went back to biting down on her lower lip.

Across the parking lot, Jeffrey had uncovered the lumber we were going to take across the island to Jeremy's shop. It looked a lot heavier than I remembered. The five of us stood around the pile, sizing up the planks.

Jeffrey broke the silence. "So . . ." he started, "here's the plan. We're going to lift the top plank and move it over to the truck, then . . ."

"I've got a better idea," Dad interrupted.

Mom bit down extra hard on her lip as she shot him a look filled with a thousand sharp daggers. She knew his plan, and she didn't approve.

"Your roof on the truck won't be strong enough to carry these. You'll dent the top. What we should do is put them on the BMW. I've got the hard top on, and it will be plenty strong."

"Steve," my mom blurted out, extending the "e" and "v" in Dad's name. "You can't do that! Do you see how *big* these planks are?"

Jeffrey stood there for a moment, considering what my dad had just offered. He was going to have to decide whether he should go with his original plan and maybe dent the roof of our truck or risk damaging his future father-in-law's pricey BMW. By now, Jeffrey knew my parents well enough to know how stubborn my dad is once his mind is made up.

"Well, that's one option, but my idea was to carry them over to the truck and place them so that they're resting on the back of the tailgate and the roof. I don't think it will be a problem," Jeffrey explained.

"If you put them on like that, don't you run the risk of the lower ends dragging on the pavement?" Dad asked.

"Hmm. I really don't think so," Jeffrey replied.

I could see that Jeffrey was in a bind and my dad had an idea that he was going to hold onto like a pit bull. I spoke up.

"You know, Jeffrey, Dad *did* drive a three-piece sectional couch on this car for eighty-five miles up I- 5 to our house. It's his car and he doesn't seem to care that he might crack the windshield. Besides, he sells these things, and he thinks the car can take it. If anything, it'll be fun to find out."

Jeffrey could see the humor in what my dad was proposing—and that strapping these huge planks on to the roof of a BMW had a high probability of damaging the roof of my dad's car. The plus side of it was that if anything happened to the car, it wouldn't be his fault. He looked over at the truck and then at the BMW and shrugged his shoulders. "Okay, fine, lets take this one over to the BMW."

We got the first plank over to the car. Getting it up onto the roof was moderately difficult.

"Are we ready for the next one?" Dad asked, walking back proudly to the stack of wood. He was happy and it showed. He'd gotten his way.

"Steve, are your really sure want to put another one on?" Mom spoke up.

Rick turned to me. "This'll be good," he laughed under his breath. "Your dad's gonna crack the window of that car."

Dad ignored Mom's protest. He had an inner glow and a smile that meant that he was pushing the envelope, and in the end he'd show us that he was right and we were all way too cautious.

With the second plank loaded and tied down, it was time to drive the mile and a half to Jeremy's shop.

I hesitated going in the car with Dad. While I loved this car, I felt rather foolish driving around Lopez Island in a convertible BMW with two sixteen-foot-long planks tied to the top, especially when we had a perfectly good working truck.

I got into the car with the same feelings I'd had in junior high school after Dad built a "camper" for his Toyota pickup truck. The camper was a big unpainted plywood box. There were two Plexiglas windows on either side near the front of the camper. At night, the sides of the camper could fold out like wings, forming bunks that were covered with a thick green nylon. It was all attached to the camper with Velcro, my dad's favorite construction material. My sister, Leigh, and I usually rode in the bed of the truck with our backs up against the rear window. I was terrified to fall asleep, afraid that I would die of carbon monoxide poisoning. It was embarrassing in junior high school to be seen in a truck with a home-built camper, and now it was just as embarrassing to be seen in a glitzy BMW that was being used like an old workhorse.

"Turn here," Jeffrey instructed my dad from the back seat.

I looked back to see if Mom and Rick were still behind us in the truck.

"You'll probably want to go slow," Jeffrey suggested.

Dad nodded, then made the turn onto the long dirt road that leads to Jeremy's shop. Dad had his left arm out the window with his hand on one of the planks.

The pothole-riddled road to Jeremy's is painful if you are driving an expensive German sports car with several hundred pounds of Douglas fir strapped to its roof. Dad expertly maneuvered through each bump in the road. I guess all the race car driving lessons he'd taken must have helped. As we crawled along, I again noticed that I'd adopted my mom's lip-biting habit as I leaned forward, up against the windshield, to watch the lumber for movement and the window for cracks.

When we pulled into Jeremy's shop, Dad was beaming. He was right.

Jeffrey was in a hurry to get started with the planer. Planers were new to me. I didn't know they existed until a couple months before and had never used one. Neither had anyone else, except Jeffrey. Dad and Rick at least knew what one was.

A planer, it turns out, is a necessary wooden-boatbuilding item. Its primary function, it appeared to me, was to turn a plank of really expensive wood into really expensive wood chips. The real purpose is to make a plank of wood an even thickness. This particular planer was heavy duty and old, and it could be fed a piece of wood that was fifteen inches wide. It had a long feed table on the inlet side and another on the outlet side. There was also a steering-wheel-like handle to raise or lower a set of cutters.

The idea is to take a plank of wood and feed it through the machine. When the wood contacts the cutters, they shave the plank a tiny bit. Jeffrey demonstrated how we could use the handle to set the amount of wood to take off. He next assigned us positions so that after we had pushed the whole plank into the planer, there would be someone to catch it on the outlet side. "The trick," he said, "is to avoid snipping the end off the plank. We'll run the same plank through the planer repeatedly until the entire thing is the thickness we want."

Another thing about planers is that they are loud. Very loud.

"Okay, so does everyone have their hearing protectors and safety glasses?" Jeffrey said as he started up the planer. He stayed on the inlet side, and we lined up behind him. As the plank went slowly through the planer, we would peel off one by one and run to the outlet side to hold up the plank as it came out. Jeffrey used hand signals to indicate whether we needed to guide the plank to the left or right, because talking was impossible over the din of the machine.

We worked until he was satisfied that both pieces of wood were the right thickness. Then we loaded the planks on the BMW and headed back to the boat. I was still apprehensive, but we made it safely to the *David B* with no perceptible damage to the car and two beautifully planed planks of wood ready to be brought on board.

As we continued to cross Whiskey Golf and the Straits of Georgia, Jeffrey and I reminisced about the early days of rebuilding the boat and my dad's uncanny ability to get away with the sketchiest scenarios. It was fun to remember back to our first days with the boat and how, at the time, we didn't think we were getting into an eight-year-long project that was to be filled with one obstacle after another.

"Yeah, your dad sure is something. Remember how much he used to love to come out to Lopez?" Jeffrey said.

"Yeah, we used to get tons of help from my family when it was on Lopez, but the moment we brought the boat to Bellingham, it wasn't so much fun for them anymore." I ended the conversation as we neared picture-perfect Lasqueti Island with its tan-barked madrone trees clinging to sandstone bluffs.

"They say that if you go to Lasqueti, don't tell Customs on the way back," Sean said.

"Really? Why?" asked Jeffrey.

"There's evidently a lot of pot growing going on there," Sean said. He carefully pulled a needle through a dock line on which he was making a whipping, then looked out the door at the island.

"We anchored over on the other side of the island with the *Schooner Zodiac* a couple of years ago. It didn't seem unusual then," Jeffrey said.

Jeffrey had wanted to explore Lasqueti at some point and was kind of disappointed to learn that there might be a problem with his plan.

"Well, I don't know if it's true or not. It's just what I heard," Sean said as Jeffrey steered us through Lasqueti's Bull Passage.

We motored along the shore of Texada Island for several hours. It seemed as if the island would never end. The glint of harbor porpoises breaking the surface in the warm afternoon light made me feel as if we could go on forever. From my seat on the bridge deck, I could look down into the water and see thousands of small jellyfish slowly pulsating with the current. Jeffrey wanted dinner to happen soon so that when it got dark we could run without any lights on in the pilothouse.

So, what's for dinner? I wondered, as I stood in the galley. *Some poached halibut, roasted potatoes, leafy greens, and bread. I can have that done by dark.*

"How much wood have you burned so far today?" Jeffrey asked as he leaned over the partial wall that separates the bridge deck from the galley. He had a mug in his hand and wanted me to fill it up with water.

"I don't know. Maybe four or five banana boxes full." I tried to remember how many times I'd gone below to get more wood.

"That seems like a lot. When I worked on the schooners in Maine, I'm sure the cooks burned a lot less. Do you think you're running the stove efficiently?" Jeffrey was trying to be helpful, but it sounded more like he was meddling.

"I don't know. I've only run the stove a few times and I'm just getting used to all the air flow vents and keeping the fire going. Maybe it seems like a lot since we have softwood here, but in Maine, the cooks probably used hardwood," I replied, not feeling happy about his line of questioning.

"You'll want to keep track of how much wood you're going through each day." He paused. "How much wood do we have on board?"

"I think we have a total of forty-two banana boxes down in the wood bin and another thirty-five or forty boxes in the Keta cabin up forward. I'm sure we'll have enough to get to Ketchikan, but we might have to find some more firewood for the stretch between Ketchikan and Juneau," I said.

"Hmmm. Well, see if you can run the stove on three or four boxes a day."

"Yeah, I'll do what I can." I handed him back the coffee mug full of water.

The stove is a joy to work with. I love the heat that radiates from it and that its top has a full spectrum of possible temperatures. If I need to melt butter, I just set a small pan on the corner of the stove farthest away from the firebox. The butter melts but doesn't get too hot or burn. When I need to boil water, I can do so without having to wait for the bull's-eye to get hot, like I have to with my electric stove at home. My Heartland Sweetheart is always ready.

For years, I had walked past the Chimney Sweep in Bellingham and peered in at the brand-new wood cookstoves made by Heartland. The stoves were white, black, green, or red with a rounded strip of shiny chrome lining the stovetop and all the doors. Just looking at them made me feel warm.

We had always planned to have a wood cookstove on the *David B*. When we bought the boat, the stove on board was an old Shipmate. We toyed with the idea that we could fix up its firebox and make repairs to the oven, but in the end we realized that it was too small for cooking for six passengers and two or three crew members. We kept the Shipmate in our backyard for a long time.

Jeffrey and I searched for the right stove for years and even made a foray down to Portland to visit Buck's Stove Palace, where we looked at hundreds of reconditioned stoves from the 1920s or 1930s. But when it came time to buy a stove, the one at the Chimney Sweep was the one I loved the most. The only problem with it was its price tag: $5,000.

Aaron, Jeffrey, and I stood inside the Chimney Sweep. I wanted the Heartland Sweetheart. I loved the stove, even though I hated the name. Sweetheart was just too sappy for a tomboy like myself. The stove's chrome glimmered. I opened and closed the oven door four or five times, feeling the quality of the construction. Above the stovetop was a wide backsplash and bread warmer connected by chrome braces. Again, I opened and closed the oven door. It was perfect, and I even liked the low chrome stand with its claw-foot legs gracefully curving outward.

Jeffrey knew I was sold on it. Aaron didn't seem to care all that much. The trip to look at the stove was just a break from work, since to him cooking was something you did to end the bad feeling of being hungry. A box of macaroni and cheese with cubes of Spam was fast and "poundable," as he liked to refer to the kind of food he enjoyed eating. Aaron had, however, gone a little foodie lately with the addition of Sriracha chili sauce to his Kraft Macaroni & Cheese.

As I looked over the stove, I imagined what it would be like to cook on and where it would sit in the pilothouse. The store's owner watched us look at the stove for a while and eventually came over to us to answer some questions. He's a tall, gaunt man who always wears black.

"That stove there, it's a quality stove, made by Mennonites in Ontario, Canada," he began to point out the details of the Sweetheart.

I looked over at Jeffrey and tried to come up with a good rationale for spending so much money on a stove. Jeffrey asked for the dimensions and what kind of heat shield we would need to install it safely. We needed to go back to the boat to see where it would fit and whether we had enough clearance for it.

"I think it would be stunning as you looked into the pilothouse for the first time," I started my sales pitch to Jeffrey and Aaron as we left the store. "I'm sure it cooks fine. Just wish it weren't so much money."

"You know you can get a gas version that doesn't need firewood that will have to be carted down the dock between each trip," Aaron spoke up.

"Yeah, I saw that, too. It does seem like it would be a lot easier, but the ambience of wood is so much nicer," Jeffrey said, thinking back to his schooner days in Maine and how much he loved to come down to the wood-heated galley after standing in the fresh air for hours.

While Jeffrey and Aaron discussed wood versus gas, I started thinking about how we could come up with the money to buy the stove. I had a pathetic little stock account that my grandfather had set up for me when I was a kid to teach me about the glories of the stock market. It had about four thousand dollars in it. We just needed to figure out how to get that last thousand so we could have the Sweetheart.

"Hey guys, I was thinking that I could sell the stock I have." I was determined to get the stove. "We'd only need to come up with about a thousand more dollars to buy that Sweetheart."

"I don't know, Christine. I think we should spend some more time looking around at reconditioned ones." Jeffrey was still not totally sold on the stove.

"The Heartland is the perfect stove for us. If we put it just opposite of the door to the galley, people will look inside and be awed by all of its bling. We need a really nice stove. It's sort of like the heart and soul of the boat. It needs to be beautiful. Just think about it. The galley is where our passengers will spend most of their time." I wasn't quite to pleading yet, but I felt like I was coming close.

"It is nice that it has all the EPA efficiency standards," Jeffrey said a few moments later. "Let's think about it some more before we make a decision."

A few days later, we drove to Kirkland to have dinner with my family. It's nice to have a big project like the *David B* to talk about, because otherwise we would have to talk about my grandfather's latest medical issues. Instead we talked about the stove I wanted. I told Grandpa how I thought I'd use the money from the stock account he had set up for me. I reasoned that it was a good use of the money, and that I should probably use it now since the stock market had been declining so much.

Grandpa's wife, Fran, listened to our story about the stove and asked us a lot of questions. I just thought she was keeping Grandpa from talking about his bowels.

"What a wonderful project you have," Fran said in her sweet raspy voice as Jeffrey and I got ready to drive back home. "I just love how busy you are. You two are really something special."

"Thanks, Fran. It's nice to hear you say that. That goes a long way. The *David B* is such a big thing; we sometimes need a little encouragement." I gave her a big hug.

On the way home we decided that I would sell my stock in the morning, and when the check arrived we'd order the stove. We could use a credit card for the remaining thousand.

A week went by, and I waited impatiently for the check. Every day I made a trip to the post office. Finally, the check from the stockbroker arrived. I tore it open and wanted to dance with excitement. We could order the stove today! There was another small envelope in the mail that day. It was from Fran. It wasn't my birthday or Jeffrey's, so it seemed a little unusual for her to send me a letter. I tore open the letter.

> Dear Christine and Jeffrey,
>
> You two work so hard. It is such a joy to listen to your stories about the boat. I have wanted to help contribute to your boat project for a long time. I hope this helps you buy the stove.
>
> With Love,
> Fran

She had written a check for one thousand dollars. Tears welled up in my eyes, and I tried not to cry in the post office. I gathered my mail and walked quickly out to the car and rushed to the boat to show Jeffrey what Fran had given us.

When the halibut was ready, I served my first "underway" dinner. Sean and I sat for dinner at the table while Jeffrey and Aaron ate on the bridge deck. We crossed Shearwater Passage and cruised past Savary Island. After dinner was finished, I cleaned up the galley, poured myself a cup of tea, turned off the lights, and joined everyone else on the bridge deck.

I enjoy being underway at night. The only light inside the pilothouse is the muted glow from the GPS, radar, and depth sounder. When my eyes adjust to looking outside, the stars and arms of the Milky Way shine with a crisp brilliance. At night, most of the boats that you see are workboats with their red and green lights marking their way through the darkness.

In the pitch black, we entered Desolation Sound. It was late when we made Galley Bay.

"You want to get ready to anchor?" Jeffrey turned to Aaron.

"Sean, can you grab the spotlight and have a look around the bay? I don't want to miss anything." Jeffrey motioned to a cabinet where the handheld spotlight lives.

Once more, Jeffrey turned to the chart plotter to look at the spot he planned to drop the anchor. He stood near the wheel and zoomed in on his picture on the radar.

"The bay looks empty, Captain," Sean reported after a quick sweep with the spotlight.

"Roger that," Jeffrey replied, and guided the *David B* to its anchorage.

"One shot," Jeffrey called out to Aaron, and the next moment, Galley Bay filled with the rattling sound of anchor chain rushing to the bottom.

We stood on deck watching and waiting for the boat to settle into place and to line up with the current. We were one day closer to our destination, and it had been a good one without drama.

"Hey, Aaron, we're finished with engines. Whenever you're ready, shut her down," Jeffrey's voice came through the darkness from the pilothouse.

I walked back to the cooler to get our ration of end-of-the-day beers. Jeffrey switched the lights on in the pilothouse. I squinted for a couple moments until my eyes adjusted to the light.

"Welcome to Galley Bay. Good job today, guys." Jeffrey was proud of us and happy with how well the boat had run.

Aaron took his beer from me and slid comfortably into the back corner of the settee. Sean and Jeffrey followed suit. I pulled up a stool and placed it close to the wood stove.

"I love how comfy this galley turned out." Jeffrey looked around the galley, taking in all that we had accomplished. "I'd almost forgotten what a mess it used to be back here. Just a big dark plywood cave, stacked with rusting tools. Remember how your mom couldn't quite figure out why we thought this would be such a great space?"

"Yeah, she has a hard time with visualization. Without any windows or a table back here, she just couldn't get the picture," I said and thought back to how ugly this space had been for so many years. Just an unpainted plywood box with water stains running down the sides.

"It was nice that there wasn't anything back here when we brought the stove down to the boat," Aaron pitched in.

"Oh yeah, that's right." Jeffrey laughed. "We cut out that hole in the back wall that would eventually be where the windows are now. It was really lucky that the box that the stove came in ended up being proportional to the size of the windows. Which, by the way, turned out awesome. Aaron, you did a good job on those windows," he said, then took a long sip of his beer.

Aaron tipped his beer to Jeffrey. "That stove was a bitch to get in here. What a pain in the ass, wheeling it down the dock and then lifting it onto the boat and then up and through the cutout. I was sure we'd drop the whole fucking thing on my feet." Aaron finished his beer. "Anyone want another?"

Jeffrey, Sean, and I each did a beer check by lifting, swirling, and then nodding. Aaron went outside for more.

"Come on, Aaron. Wasn't the assembly and positioning of the stove fun?" I asked.

"Oh, yeah. That was good, too, dragging it all around the pilothouse until we broke the damn thing's legs," Aaron replied through the open window in the back of the pilothouse.

"Well, that turned out to have been a good thing. Those legs weren't strong enough to be on a boat. The setup we have now is a lot better," Jeffrey said.

"Did your friend Greg weld up that stand?" Sean asked.

"Yeah. Once he got back from cruising to Hawaii, he made the new base, and then he got started on all the cabinetry in here," Jeffrey said, opening up his second beer.

"What was the first thing you cooked on the stove?" Sean asked me.

"Oh, it was 'Aaron food'—grilled cheese sandwiches and chocolate-chip cookies. I tried to make the cookies extra big for Aaron, but I hadn't figured out how to control the temperature, so the first batch turned out a little overdone on the outside and a little raw in the middle." I opened my second beer and shifted my stool closer to the stove.

"It's a cool stove, but it's still a major pain in the ass to move all that wood down into the engine room," Aaron reminded me.

"You're right. It totally sucks, but it feels so good to sit next to it." I leaned in closer to absorb some more heat.

"Hey, guys," Jeffrey interrupted from where he was resting comfortably in the back of the settee. "Sorry to change the subject, but Christine, what time do we need to get to Yuculta Rapids?"

"I don't know. I think it's twelve-thirty or one, maybe, but you had better check," I said, getting up to find the current tables and a calculator for him.

"Do we get to sleep in?" Aaron's face lit up with the prospect of a full night's sleep.

"Looks that way," Jeffrey said, after finding the entry for Seymour Narrows currents and doing a few calculations to get the time for slack water at Yuculta Rapids.

I emptied my beer and looked at my watch. It was just after midnight and time for bed. I got up to go outside for a few minutes. Aaron left for his bunk, happy for the chance to sleep in. Sean and Jeffrey continued talking in the galley.

The yellow glow of light that spilled out of the pilothouse and into the inky darkness made me feel warm and safe. The still air held on to the smell of muskeg and felt cool on my cheeks. I could hear the wind in the trees up on the ridge top, but down here in the sheltered bay, it was perfectly still. I breathed in the air and sat silently for a while with my back up against the pilothouse, thinking of nothing, simply enjoying life.

There's a bittersweet emotion that comes with the realization of a goal. I'd become addicted to the chaos of progress. At the time I hated that chaos, but I now knew how much I was going to miss it.

I smiled to myself, remembering back to all those cold days and nights we had spent working on the boat. Not long after we brought the boat to Bellingham, we had to remove the rest of the deck planking and deck beams. We were quick to replace the beams, but then for years, we walked on naked deck beams as we worked on the boat, trying our best to keep up with all the rot and decay that permeated the *David B.*

My mom decided early in the rebuild that Jeffrey and I had not really bought a boat, but a pattern for a boat. She was sure that what we were doing was carefully removing each part of the boat, making a copy of it, and replacing it.

I leaned my head back against the pilothouse and stared up at the stars. Everything, with the exception of the shell of the pilothouse, was new. The cabinetry, the floor, the deck, and the beams the deck sits on are new. The cushions were made by my sister, my mom, and myself. The table and settee were built by our friend Greg. Sean did all the decorative carving. Aaron and Jeffrey laid the pretty fir decking on top of the plywood. Then Aaron spent a couple of days sanding the flooring down before I finished it with deck oil. Aaron's dad and an electrician friend, Danny, did the wiring, and I painted. It was a group effort to rebuild the *David B*. Jeffrey and I could never have done it on our own.

I was beginning to realize that a chapter of my life had come to an end. These last few months before we left for Alaska had been quite festive. Our house, the shop, and the boat bustled with activity. I made big meals in the evenings, and there were always conversations going on late into the night. I would miss waking up in the morning and tip-toeing around the sleeping bags of friends and shipwrights that often stretched from the front door and into the kitchen. Our recycling bin would no longer be piled so embarrassingly high with beer cans that it looked like that of a frat house. It had been a great time of my life, and I'd never forget those days.

Now that all the shipwrights and friends except Sean had gone, we'd had to shift our goal from restoring an old rotten boat to operating a successful business. This new goal was turning out to be much more difficult. Neither Jeffrey nor I have much experience in marketing, and Aaron is not interested in the business side of the boat. It scared me to think about what little time and how little money we had to fill the boat with passengers before we ran out of money. I sighed in the dark.

Stop fretting about the money situation. Enjoy this beautiful night. You've put in a lot of effort into being here. Now forget about the future for a moment. I breathed in and relaxed my body against the pilothouse. I felt as if I could have melted myself deep into the old wood of the boat, where its ancient timbers would, from now on, take care of me. The *David B* was a part of me, and that would never change.

CHAPTER 4

TIME SEEMED TO STAND STILL

M/V David B -- Ship's Log   Date _21 JUNE 2006_

Time	Location	Wind	Baro	Depth	Remarks
0440	Anchored Gatley Bay	Calm	1026	31 ft	Clear
0830	U/W From Ganley Bay				
1648	ANCHORED THURSTON BAY			38 ft	Clutch Slipping
2000	BEAR ON BEACH				

"WHERE ARE YOU GOING? It's so nice and warm here in the bed. We can sleep in," Jeffrey complained to me at five the next morning.

"It's way too beautiful of a morning to stay in bed. I'm going to start the stove and make some muffins. Have you seen my spotting scope?"

"Over there somewhere." He motioned toward the back of the cabin.

I rummaged around and found the scope. "I love you, Jeffrey. I'll be back down with some coffee in an hour or so. Sleep well." I turned around, kissed Jeffrey, ran my free hand through his hair, then tucked the covers under his chin.

"Mmmm," Jeffrey said, and fell back into a deep sleep.

I climbed up into the galley, then walked out onto the deck. It would be a while before the sun cleared the hills and dried up the dew. I immediately spotted two marbled murrelets. The sound of the pilothouse door startled them, and in the same instant, they dove, leaving nothing but two ripples radiating across the surface.

Wow, what a way to start the morning. Those little birds have become so scarce. I set up my spotting scope. I would have to wait until I got the stove going before I'd really have time to watch the birds. For the moment, I stood and watched the ripples diffuse into the mirrored calm of the water.

Back inside the galley, I got the stove started, and the muffins were soon in the oven. I ground the coffee beans and prepared my French presses. *There's no such thing as strong coffee, only weak people.* I laughed to myself, thinking about how much I liked a good, strong cup of coffee first thing in the morning.

It was warming up out on deck, and I went outside to sit with my coffee and spotting scope. The cove was now abuzz with rufous hummingbirds that zipped around the boat. They came to inspect everything that was painted red and seemed especially taken with the handles on the windlass.

The marbled murrelets were still nearby and continued to feed around the boat. These small mottled brown birds have long commutes between their nests and the saltwater bays where they forage. The few nests that have been found are often on high branches of trees in old-growth forests up to 45 miles inland. It's no wonder there are so few left—there's no place for them. Their habitat has been turned into houses, paper, and our boat. I watched the murrelets diving and surfacing while the sun climbed higher over the hillside and warmed my face.

✻

We'd been running for an hour or so, northbound in Homfray Channel. When Jeffrey leaned over the wall that separates the bridge deck from the galley. "Come check this out. This place is just incredible. I've wanted to show it to you for a long time. What do you think?"

I stepped up to the bridge deck and stood next to Jeffrey. "I think it's amazing. The sides of this fjord are so steep and the waterfalls so high that they seem to pour from the sky."

"The mountain up there, Mount Grazebrooke, is the one that I drew for you when I came up here on *Schooner Zodiac* without a camera. I knew you would love this place." Jeffrey smiled and put his arm around me.

"You're right, and I wish we could spend more time here." I was a little overwhelmed by beauty of Homfray Channel.

As we traveled, we hugged the west shore of the channel. At times Jeffrey took us right along the steep cliff faces, sometimes as close as twenty or thirty feet away. I felt I could almost reach out and touch the rocks. I decided to take a nap, so I went up to the foredeck, lay down on my stomach, and soaked up the warmth on my belly.

We began our restoration of the *David B* by removing the foredeck. On our first day, we arrived on Lopez early, armed with crowbars, a couple of hammers, a Skilsaw, a Sawzall, and a lot of enthusiasm.

Jeffrey stood at the port bow of the boat. "Well, here it goes," he said, and kneeled down to the deck. I stood over him and watched as he swung the prying end of his hammer. It made a dead thud into the soft wood. He pulled the hammer back again and swung.

"Ready for a crowbar?" I stood with the smaller one in my hand.

"How about the Skilsaw instead," he said.

Jeffrey made the opening cut and then pried out the first foot of decking. He handed me the hammer and small crowbar, then explained a couple tricks for removing the deck planks. I went to work while Jeffrey moved aside to begin opening up the starboard side of the deck.

Our crowbars dug easily into the planking and tore up the soft wood, ripping and splintering old rotten decking and tar-coated plywood. The Sawzall was hungry that day. Its vibration in my hands was like the purr of a satisfied cat after a kill. The teeth of its bi-metal blade cut through the deck like butter, only occasionally slowed by an ancient fastener.

By midday the sun was hot. I was dirty, and the T-shirt and shorts I wore were filthy. My skin was sweaty and coated red with a fine film of tar dust, sawdust, and rust dust. Under the noonday sun, I smelled like fungus, rusty nails, wood, and asphalt. That smell is forever imprinted in my mind.

As I lay on the foredeck thinking about that first day, I breathed deep, in search of that smell. It's gone now, replaced with new fir, fresh plywood, and deck oil. Sometimes I catch a whiff of that timeless smell, usually tucked in hard-go-get-to places like the anchor chain locker or the bilge. The smell of the *David B's* age lingers in its timbers, reminding me that with a wood boat, no restoration is ever complete.

Eight years ago, with my Sawzall and pry-bar, I was foolishly confident. But as we worked, doubt began to creep into my soul. *This project might be too big* fluttered across my mind as I pulled away rotten deck and watched Jeffrey's body language. *Nah, Jeffrey knows what we're doing. It's going to be all right. We'll get this done*, I reassured myself even as I noted that with each cut of the saw, we found more and more rot.

Where we thought we could simply remove the tarred plywood and sand down the original decking, we discovered that there was nothing underneath we could save. We held out for months that some of the planks near the mast were sound.

As we removed the deck planking and exposed the tops of the deck beams, we discovered that they too, were rotten and would need to be removed and replaced. Late in the afternoon on the first day, I stood on the main deck next to the bone pile of deck planks and beams.

"Hey, what are we going to do with all this wood?" I called out to Jeffrey, who was down below.

"Jeremy said we could put it over on his burn pile on the shore," he replied from low in the anchor-chain locker.

"Everything OK down there?" I peered down into the opening where the deck had been.

"Yeah, I think so, but I'm afraid we're going to have to remove the beam shelf as well. It's pretty far gone," he said, with a mix of disappointment and conviction.

I picked up an armload of wood and headed to the beach. *Two years to have the boat ready. I sure hope we don't find anything else wrong.*

The following weekend, Jeffrey and I sat in the line for the ferry to Lopez when we heard a news story that angry protesters were picketing Home Depot hardware stores for selling old-growth lumber. "Hmmm." We looked at each other as we listened to the report on the radio.

"What do you bet Home Depot sells old-growth a lot cheaper than our boat lumber distributor?" Jeffrey said. "We could save a whole lot of cash liberating old-growth timber from some poorly constructed do-it-yourselfer's kitchen remodel."

"Yeah, maybe we should head over there this week to see what they've got before it gets pulled from the shelves—or even worse, some other boat builder gets it." I smiled and wrote Home Depot on my to-do list.

A few days later, as we got in the truck, I confessed to Jeffrey, "You know, I feel like I'm somehow betraying my environmental morals by buying old-growth Douglas fir. Am I going to environment hell where I'm forced to watch terrible things done to cute furry woodland creatures for all of eternity?"

"No, it's not wrong. Think of it as rescuing this beautiful wood from the degradation of being used as studs for walls in housing developments. The crime is not that the old-growth is used—it's how its being used. Old-growth should be used in such a way that it shows, like an heirloom table or chair, or a wooden boat. It doesn't belong in the Sheetrocked walls of houses where no one knows it's there. That's where the crime is."

We walked through the double-wide doors of the Home Depot and grabbed one of the hard-to-push orange carts that wobble on shopping-cart-like wheels and pushed it to the lumber section. We stopped in front of the stack of four-by-fours.

"Hey, Christine, come help me lift these," Jeffrey said, pointing to the sixteen-foot stack. "Can you wipe the owl feathers off the top ones?" he laughed.

It took about forty-five minutes to cherry-pick through the wood. The price was substantially lower than from the specialty lumber store in Port Townsend. We took our treasure to the checkout counter. Each four-by-four we found was beautiful and would make a strong deck. I can't say that I was proud of our purchase, but I was happy to rescue this wood from an eternity hidden in the walls of a bland subdivision.

"When I go to the island this week, I'll have Ken help me unload them," Jeffrey suggested as we loaded our truck in the parking lot.

"Yeah, it would be good to get a little work out of him, so he's not just living on the boat for free," I replied, thinking about the odd arrangement we had with the guy who came with the boat.

When we bought the boat, it came with Ken. We inherited him from Jeremy, who had allowed him to live aboard the *David B* in return for a small number of hours of work each month. Our newly acquired liveaboard, like the handful of other "cash-only" people in this little neighborhood of old rotten boats, didn't give up too much about himself. The name he went by was Ken, but we've always referred to him as "The Guy That Came with the Boat." He was part of a loose community of liveaboards and artists that was peppered with a collection of somewhat transient first-name-only people. Ken was the self-proclaimed Mayor of Shoal Bay.

He was tall and slender, with dark hair and a drinking problem, and he had a knack for avoiding my camera. He talked using the metric system and had a military background. Over the years we have made up dozens of stories about who he really was.

As the weeks passed, Jeffrey grew more and more frustrated with the limitations of our operation at Lopez. It was difficult for us having Ken living on the boat, since he was occupying the only livable space. For us to spend a weekend working on the boat, we would have to sleep outside on deck. We talked about asking him to move, but he was always helpful, and we knew that he would take care of the boat when we couldn't be there.

Another problem with having the boat at Lopez was that it took three hours of travel each way to get there, and that severely limited the amount of work we could get done. There was also a lack of covered work space. When it rained, we got wet, and our power tools did, too.

"Fuck!" Jeffrey exclaimed while making a saw cut.

"You all right?" I looked up. Rain was cascading off my hat.

"Yeah, I just got a shock. This whole setup is killing us." Jeffrey kept working.

The way in which we got electricity to the boat was taxing on the tools, so when it rained, it really brought down our moods. A long power cord ran from a building 500 feet away to a small outbuilding. Inside there was an outlet from which an extension cord was strung over the water to the boat. The end of that extension cord had been rewired to attach an outlet box at the end and was protected from the rain by a plastic milk jug cut in half and tied around it.

One evening Jeffrey came home fuming about the difficulty of accomplishing anything on Lopez. He'd spent the whole day working on deck beams.

"So get this," he said, storming around the kitchen. "I was happily working away on the number-three deck beam when this old guy came up to me and started asking a bunch of questions. That was fine. I didn't have a problem with that, but then—I couldn't believe it. He just dusted off the deck beam I was working on and sat his retired old-guy butt right down on my work. It was a totally malicious act. Doesn't he know I only have five, maybe six hours of actual work I can get done in a day? He seriously just sat down on my deck beam and didn't budge for a good half hour. He just kept on going, 'blah, blah, blah,' and 'back in my day,' and 'when I was in the Navy' and on and on and on. When I'd motion that I wanted to get back to work, he'd come up with some other story to tell me. We've got to finish up that deck project so we can get the boat to Bellingham. Our whole damn project will be old-guyed to death by retired Lopezians with nothing to do."

"Wow, did he really dust off the beam first?" I imagined Jeffrey trying to get some work done.

"Yes, he actually did give the beam a quick swoosh with his hand before he sat his butt right where I was trying to work. It was goddamned infuriating. All I wanted to do was work on my beam, but he wouldn't let me. We've got to get a sign that says something like 'No Old Guys' or 'Please Leave Us Alone. We Are Trying To Get Something Fucking Done Here.'"

"Well Jeffrey, I think old guys come with the territory. You've got something going on and that poor fellow, he's probably just lonely and wants someone to talk to. I bet his wife made him leave the house for a couple of hours because, ever since he retired, he's been driving her crazy. So just think about it. He's already hit up all his buddies and nothing new's going on. He spots you doing something in the open, so you're fair game. Don't worry. Someday you'll get your chance to old-guy some young kid. Think of this guy as a mentor."

I love teasing Jeffrey about his intolerance of old guys. Besides, he already exhibits old-guy tendencies at the grocery store checkout line by asking the clerks too many questions about tabloid headlines.

My time for napping and reminiscing was almost over. I soaked up the sun for a few more minutes, lying on the deck and watching the world slowly pass by at six and a half knots. I shifted my right arm under my chin so I could watch the hypnotic curl of water along the hull of the boat as the sun shone down on my back. As we cruised this back channel away from Desolation Sound, the image of a picture taken of me and my mom standing in the galley together drifted across my mind. My dad had snapped the picture in the late fall while the *David B* was still at Lopez. Jeffrey and I had recently gotten engaged, and my mom had agreed to make my wedding dress. Whenever they would come to help us work on the boat, Mom would bring a special box that held a mock-up pattern of my dress made from a bunch of old bedsheets.

"Okay, stop what you're doing and come into the galley. It's time to try on your dress," she would announce, and then add, with a twinge of doubt in her voice, "I sure hope I get this done in time."

I'd drop everything, including my pants, to put the dress on so she could make adjustments. As fall turned into winter, stripping down to my undies to try on a dress made of old white sheets became a lot less pleasant.

"Hold still," Mom would say.

"I'm trying to, but your fingers are cold," I'd complain as she would take in some fabric near my bare shoulders.

"If you keep shivering, I'm going to stick you with a pin," she'd say through her teeth while holding three or four pins tightly between her lips.

There wasn't much room to move around in the galley the way Ken had it set up. Mom moved cautiously, making marks and pinning fabric. She was careful not to bump the table and knock down the framed coins Ken had collected on military excursions to the Middle East.

"This is what you get for asking me to make your wedding gown." She'd laugh as her cold fingers brushed against my skin when she helped lift the dress over my head.

I loved that Mom had taken the time to make my dress. Even with all the frustration of working on Lopez Island, our work created a festive feeling. I glanced up from the curl of water along the boat's hull. Homfray Channel was wide here, and a floating logging camp was moored to the other shore.

In the fall of 1998, we had a pretty good routine going. Jeffrey's summer boat-driving job had switched to winter outfitting, and he was now on a Monday-through Friday-schedule. Early on Saturday mornings, we would load up the truck with a foam mattress and supplies for the weekend and take the earliest ferry to the island. We had started sleeping in the truck because it was too cold to sleep on deck. We had a Coleman camp stove and we'd bring our own water. Lunch was mostly ramen noodles or Kraft Macaroni & Cheese. Dinner was often the same.

We had finished making the beam shelf and the deck beams. Each one was slightly different. They all had to be cut out with a slight rise in the middle, or camber as the boat builders call it, to allow water to run off the deck when it rained or in rough seas. It was fun making the deck beams. Jeffrey would carefully measure out the shape of the new beam and draw it onto a six-by-twelve length of Douglas fir. Then he'd fire up his chainsaw and rough out the beam. My job was to plane it smooth by shaving off the surface, one sixty-fourth of an inch of wood at a time, down to the lines Jeffrey had drawn. We worked on the deck beams on shore. When one was finished, we'd haul in the swing float and carefully walk it over to the *David B*, where we'd secure the beam to the beam shelf.

As the months went by, our pile of new wood ashore got smaller, and the grime that washed down the drain when we came home to shower was slowly being replaced by the scent of freshly sawn Douglas fir. It was the smell of progress.

One Sunday afternoon, Jeremy came by the boat and took Jeffrey aside.

"I heard that you guys have been sleeping on shore, in your truck," he said.

"Yeah, it makes it a lot easier for us."

"Well, we can't have that. You know, if others started doing that, the property owners might decide we can't use this parking lot any more, and we've got a pretty good thing going here," Jeremy said.

"Sure, not a problem," Jeffrey said, not concealing his disappointment.

We still had Ken living on the *David B*, and neither one of us really wanted to share the pilothouse with him. Not that he was a bad guy; it just seemed weird.

"It's always about the Haves versus the Have-Nots," Jeffrey stewed after Jeremy had left. "In this case, it's *hippies* that have against *hippies* that have-not. They won't let us use the parking lot to sleep in any more because they're all worried that the hippies that have not might invade, and they'll lose their access to the parking lot."

"That's just another obstacle to make things a little more difficult. Why do you think they care? They know we'll be gone soon. You'd think the owners would set up a god-dammed yurt for us, since we're about to remove one of Shoal Bay's biggest eyesores," I was mad. It seemed like such a trivial thing to worry about. We were low-key and trying our best to get off the island.

"Yeah, I agree with you. I think Jeremy mentioned one time that Ken has small a boat over by the wharf building. It might be time for him to start moving his stuff over there so we can stay on the *David B*. I'll talk with him when he gets back and give him a date to move off the boat," Jeffrey said, starting up his chainsaw for another deck beam.

We were getting close to finishing the foredeck, and friends and family were still showing up on the weekends to help. It was time to start laying the deck planking and purchasing fasteners.

Wooden boat people are crazy about fasteners. They love them, and they love to talk about them. When two wooden boat aficionados meet for the first time, they size up one another's knowledge by skillfully injecting into the conversation that such-and-such boat is held together by this-or-that kind of fastener.

Jeffrey's worth as a shipwright was riding on his choice of fasteners, and he'd put a lot of thought into what he was going use for the deck. This was agonizing for me. Every day he'd ask, "What do you think we should use on the foredeck?" and every day I'd answer, "I don't know, Jeffrey. I'm new to all this fastener stuff."

The *David B* was like a giant practicum, and I had been cramming for the test on boat fasteners. It made me dizzy to think about the innumerable ways to screw, bolt, or nail wood together, and how many different materials those solutions are made of. I was shocked to learn that Bellingham had not one but two stores that were dedicated to selling all kinds of fasteners. It didn't really surprise me that Jeffrey was dealing with a mild case of option paralysis.

After weeks of agonizing, Jeffrey finally decided on quarter-inch by four-inch galvanized lag bolts. To fasten the deck planking, we were also going to need an array of drill bits, and this, too, required careful consideration—and gave Jeffrey the opportunity to buy another drill. We would use a spade bit, an eighth-inch drill bit, and a quarter-inch drill bit to set each one.

I stood with Jeffrey in the crowded and narrow aisle of the fasteners section at Hardware Sales. We had already been there once before that day, but Jeffrey wanted to spend more time looking at washers now that he had made a decision about his lag bolts. He was unhappy with the size of quarter-inch washers. To set the bolts, we needed to sink the heads of the bolts down into holes the size of washers, and the quarter-inch washers were too big to be aesthetically pleasing when the holes were capped with bungs. He fingered through bins of washers and tested each eligible washer on one of the lag bolts.

"Hey, check this out. What do you think?" Jeffrey finally turned to me. "It's odd, but this three-sixteenth-inch washer fits the quarter-inch bolt, and it's way smaller."

I inspected the fastener combination and handed it back to Jeffrey. "That looks nice. That'll make a nice bung hole."

Once we nailed down the decision on fasteners, we next needed to work out how to get the most planking out of the raw lumber we had. I'm not really sure why there hasn't been some sort of people's revolt against the advertised size of dimensional lumber. For some reason, when you buy a four-by-four, it's really only three-and-a-half-by-three-and-a-half, and a two-by-two is really a one-and-a-half-by-one-and-a-half. If you buy an eight-by or wider piece of wood, the lumber mills tend to shave off a little bit more so your eight-by tends to be closer to a seven and a quarter. I was appalled for three reasons: First, because it seemed like a shady practice; second, because this also seemed to be one of those things that men are born knowing; and third, because they all seemed to think that the misrepresentation of a four-by-four was perfectly acceptable. Not only did this misrepresentation mean there was more math to do when trying to figure out how much wood a person might need, it also felt like we were not quite getting what we paid for.

The dimensions of lumber evidently have something to do with milled versus rough-sawn and, as Jeffrey calculated the number of planks we could get out of a four-by-four, he also had to take into account that some of our planking stock had rounded corners that would have to be sawn off.

In the end, our deck planking was going to be two-and-a-quarter inches thick by three-and-a-half inches wide. While we had scoured the Home Depot for old-growth Douglas fir, we couldn't get enough before they stopped selling it, so we made a special order from a local mill to make up the rest of the planking stock.

It was mid-January when we laid our first piece of planking. The cold prevented us from fully realizing the milestone we had just reached. Shivering next to a stack of freshly sawn deck planks, I helped Jeffrey lay out where each one would end. Their golden hue contrasted with the old, rough covering board with its beaver-like "chew" marks.

"So, what you want to do is take the drill with the spade bit and drill a hole down about an inch into the plank," Jeffrey explained to my sister Leigh and our friend Ian, who had come to help us. "Next you'll find the center of the hole, and then take the other drill with the eighth-inch drill bit to make a pilot hole. I've put a piece of tape on it to mark how deep to go. Then take the spade bit out of the first drill and put in the quarter-inch one to drill the hole for the shank. The last step is going to be kind of old school. You'll use a hand-cranked brace with a deep socket at the end to twist in the lag bolt with washer down into the hole." The three of us nodded as Jeffrey showed us the process.

I had dozed off, once again, on the warm deck as we continued through Homfray Channel. It felt good to be still for a while. It was really the first time in eight years I had taken time to relax. Between working and boat building, there was seldom any time left over for recreation. I'd pretty much given up the last few ski seasons to work on the boat, which was sad for me, but it seemed that the reward of fixing up the boat would be greater than the sacrifice of a few good turns up at Mt. Baker.

I closed my eyes again and let my mind wander back to the end of the foredeck project. With the deck nearly finished, we made plans to bring the boat to Bellingham. Jeffrey leased a slip in the commercial side of the harbor. He had also asked Michael to come out from Maine and help run the engine.

At the end of January, we felt we were almost ready to move the boat. February was already shaping up to be a hectic month on top of moving the boat. Soundings of the Planet, where I worked, had been kicked out of its neighborhood office for being too big and was moving to a business park. We had also just bought our first house, and the sale was scheduled to close in a few days. Everything was in motion.

We were worried that there might be some trouble with the engine, or the boat itself, so we arranged for our friend Loren to take us out to Lopez on his boat, the *Chief Kwina*, and to shadow us for our maiden voyage. Our friends Grant, Bill, and Ian agreed to help as well.

Loren greeted us warmly when we arrived at the *Chief Kwina*. His unique booming voice, which emphasizes every third or fourth word, filled the air. "It's awful early for work'n on a Saturday," he said stressing the "EAR" in early, before rising again to the "SAT" of Saturday.

"Good morning. Sure is," I said as I stepped aboard the *Chief*. Loren's a big guy with big fisherman's hands. They've always reminded me of bear paws, and they make a can of beer appear to have the proportions of a can of tomato paste. I first met him when he and Jeffrey were working in Seward, Alaska, trading off three-week stints on a sightseeing boat.

The *Chief Kwina's* engine was idling and the smell of diesel exhaust hung in the cold, still morning air.

"These are some good groceries," Loren said as I handed him big pot of beef stew that I had made the night before.

The rest of the crew began to arrive with coffees in hand, suffering their usual Saturday-morning hangovers and dressed in their typical workboat clothing.

There's a kind of unspoken uniform worn by professional mariners that is very different from yachting clothes. This "uniform" is actually similar to the style that construction workers wear but diverges even from that, in a couple of subtle ways. The most basic item that boat people wear is Carhartt pants, usually the canvas duck-brown color, although some women who work on tall ships might sport the white painter style. Frequently the pants have telltale spots of paint—red for bottom paint, or black, white, green, or blue for topside paint. Often there are stains from grease and oil. Wooden-boat shipwrights will sometimes wear quilted Carhartt overalls in the winter.

The shoes boat people wear are another subtle indication of their trade. On the West Coast, all pros wear the ubiquitous brown neoprene Xtratufs. These tall boots can be worn in a few important ways. The first is like a normal rubber boot: Slip them on and tuck in the pants. Fashion-conscious young females on charter boats and in fishing communities always wear their Xtratufs with very tight jeans tucked inside. Some fishermen wear sweat pants that balloon over the tops.

Another way is to roll down the tops of the boots so that they rest around the ankle. This is a more casual way of wearing the boots that's useful for walking around town when not working on the deck of a boat with water sloshing back and forth. Xtratufs are also rolled down when they're stored to help them dry out inside. Sometimes it's too much trouble to unroll the tops and the boat person just slips them on in the rolled-down state.

The last stage of life for the boots is the Xtratuf "slipper." The thrifty boat person will cut them off at the ankle and instantly have a pair of slippers. These are good for quick trips outside to take a leak over the rail when you don't want to take the time to fully put on a pair of boots. In my experience, few women wear Xtratuf slippers. However, there seems to be a small cult of fishing-community women who get together with their girlfriends and cut their boots into fashionable slippers.

The other footwear that boat people wear are called Romeos. These slip-on shoes are ankle high, with thick dark rubber soles and leather uppers, and are usually worn in dry weather. Unless you work on a fancy plastic yacht, there isn't much concern about scuffing up the decks with dark-soled shoes. You won't find topsiders in the wardrobe of the professional mariner.

Boat people's clothing also shows their allegiance to the boats they and their friends work on. As Grant, Bill, and the others arrived, they wore an assortment of jackets with the names of boat companies they had worked for. A couple of the jackets worn on the *Chief Kwina* that day were red and embroidered in blue with Major Marine Tours, the company where Jeffrey had met Loren, Grant, and Bill.

When we arrived in Shoal Bay, I took my pot of stew over to the *David B* and started up the little propane Wedgewood stove to heat up our lunch. The stove was an afterthought from the thirties or forties and had been placed close to the door in the galley. It was small, with four burners and a broken oven. I thought it was cute and figured that maybe someday we'd restore it and put it in our house. As I set out silverware, I glanced over at the wood-burning Shipmate stove that was built into the aft counter. I would like to have started it, but we were out of scrap wood and I didn't bring any extra. I stirred the stew until it was hot and stacked the bowls on the counter.

Over lunch there was talk of the work that we had done on the island. The guys asked Jeffrey questions about laying down the deck and how the engine worked. It was time to get the *David B* underway. I was a little anxious, but it comforted me that the *Chief Kwina* would be nearby if anything went wrong.

After lunch, we gathered in the engine room where Jeremy explained the quirks of the engine to Jeffrey and Michael. There was no way to shift into ahead, astern, or neutral from the pilothouse; that had to be done in the engine room by the engineer. Jeremy got out the black steel shifting bar. It was about six feet long, with a slight curve to the end. The bar needed to be put into the gearbox, somehow, and pulled down or pushed up to shift. Michael, who was going to be the engineer, gave it a shot. I watched him lean hard into it. I could tell that I wasn't strong enough to shift the engine.

Jeremy moved around the engine like a hurried leprechaun, opening valves and levers. He went to the front of the engine and began to bar the engine over, placing a shorter bar into one of the holes in the rim of the thousand-pound flywheel. He opened a small door on the side that showed the camshaft and pulled down on the bar. The first pull on the bar looked hard, but then he moved the bar and pulled again, and the flywheel seemed to loosen up. Jeffrey took over and continued to slowly turn the flywheel. He kept looking inside the open door. I couldn't see what he was looking for, but he seemed to be watching for something to line up. Each pull of the bar caused the engine to make an exhaling sound, and the sugary sweet smell of semi-combusted diesel filled the engine room.

With the barring done, Jeremy explained that the engine was ready to start. "Never leave the bar in the flywheel. If the engine starts with it in, the bar would rip though the hull like a knife in soft butter," Jeremy cautioned. The image frightened me.

From my position in the very back of the engine room, I listened to talk of oil, fuel, and air pressures. There was so much about the engine that was new to me. All I knew about diesel engines came from the diesel Volkswagen Dasher I had in college. With that engine, all I had to do was make sure the glow plug light turned green before I turned the key. There were no glow plugs on the Washington, so I sat in the back of the engine room hoping that I'd learn something that would make the engine make sense to me.

Under Jeremy's direction, Jeffrey pumped up the fuel pressure, then quickly pulled on a big red lever. The engine kicked into life. It was amazing. The previously cold, quiet green relic was now alive with moving parts and heat. On its starboard side are nine slender steel rods, each about the length of my arm. These "pushrods" moved in an up and down in mechanical step. It reminded me vaguely of the carnival game Whack-a-Mole, where moles pop up out of holes and you try to give them a good thumping on the head.

I stood near the back of the engine room, watching the men tend to the engine like worker bees to the queen. The sound from the engine was surprisingly soothing, more like an oversized sewing machine than the screaming banshees that power modern boats. The longer the engine ran, the warmer it became. Being a cat person, I suddenly realized that I liked this space. The waltz-like heartbeat of the engine was both calming and reassuring.

We prepared to get underway. The *Chief Kwina* pulled away from the *David B's* side. I was grateful that it was such a beautiful sunny day. The water was calm, and it felt more like mid-April than the first week in February. It was warm enough to be on deck in a long-sleeved flannel shirt and no jacket. I pondered the significance of our "maiden voyage" while Jeffrey and Michael worked out the bugs of their communication system. They both agreed that it was too sketchy to use the Engine Bell Code that came with the boat, so they worked out a simplified version and tested it a few times.

"OK, so, I'll ring the bell once for ahead, twice for neutral, and three times for astern." Jeffrey's eyes lit up as he reached down and rang the bell.

"Aye. That's ahead." Michael smiled. "You won't need to be changing speed, will you?"

They practiced a few times. Each time Michael took the boat in and out of gear, there was a loud snapping sound and the boat would move forward or backward. On deck, the dock lines would creak and stretch. After a few tries, Jeffrey was satisfied that their system would work.

I took hold of the bowline and waited for Jeffrey to give me the OK to let it go. I trembled a bit, hoping nothing would go wrong. I tried to suppress the worry that the boat would somehow fall apart on our journey home. It was nice knowing that we had a new emergency pump on board, which Jeffrey's parents had bought for us, and that the *Chief Kwina* would be shadowing us all the way back to Bellingham.

Everything will be just fine, I told myself over and over.

When the last line was untied, Jeffrey rang once and we slowly slid away from the dock. We were finally underway. On the *Chief Kwina,* everyone stood on deck watching us, Loren wearing his engine-room overalls and Grant and Bill with beers in hand. Jeremy, in his newsboy cap, stood up in his small wooden skiff with an old large-format camera. He was silhouetted in the low winter sun. The *David B* shook like an overly excited dog. From the bridge deck, our newly completed foredeck seemed to glow.

"Do you see that mooring buoy in front of us?" I asked. We needed to make a big U-turn to get out of the harbor, and head toward Bellingham, and the place was full of mooring buoys. Jeffrey had been turning the wheel a little to port, then a little to starboard, but for some reason the boat wasn't making the turn to get out of the harbor or avoid the buoys.

"Yeah, I see it, but something's weird with the steering," Jeffrey said nervously. "I can't tell if it's not working at all or what's wrong with it." It was the first time the steering had been used since Jeffrey had hooked it up a month ago. He turned it a full turn to starboard.

"Whoa, shit! We're turning the wrong way." He bent down, looked at the steering cables, then stood up to glance out the window. "I think I hooked the steering up backward.

"At least we're going to miss that buoy," he laughed, "but we'll go on the other side of it, I guess. As soon as we're past it, I'll try turning the wheel the other way."

I watched as we motored past the mooring. Then Jeffrey spun the wheel the other way.

"Yup, it's fucking backward. How did I do that?" He paused. "And how am I going to remember *that* when I'm trying to steer?"

"It's probably like the psychologist who wore the inverting glasses that turned his world upside down," I offered. "He learned to ride his motorcycle, didn't he?"

"Yeah, but it took him a few days, right?" he countered.

"Hey, there's another buoy in front of us," I said.

"Uh shit, um, left is right, right is left . . . I want to go that way . . . Okay, I've got it. See, I'm ready for that motorcycle already," Jeffrey said, sounding proud of his new skill.

We motored out of the harbor without any other close calls, with Jeffrey only occasionally having to mutter "Left is right, right is left, I want to go right, so . . . "

The *David B* moved through the water for the first time in who knows how long. Its thin bow sliced softly through the water, and its heavily built hull felt stable and secure. My nerves settled as I felt its sturdiness. Jeffrey seemed confident and happy. I relaxed and thought about why I was afraid of the *David B*. I guessed that it was just the fear of the unknown. I was scared that the boat would sink out from underneath us.

Should I be afraid? I wondered. *Well, no, not afraid, but maybe aware of what's going on. Will the boat sink? Probably not. It's made of wood. Wood floats, right? Will we spring a plank underwater? Maybe. What do we do if that happens? Get the pump out. That's what we'll do. Will we make it back to Bellingham? Sure we will, right?* I looked over at Jeffrey again to see if he was showing any signs of concern. If he was, he kept it to himself.

"So are you ready to go faster?" Michael asked.

"Yeah, you want to bring us up a bit," Jeffrey said.

Michael left and went down to the engine room, and the engine sped up. The boat shook a bit harder with the new speed.

"Do you hear that?" Jeffrey asked Ian.

"No, what?" Ian replied.

"That shhh-shh-shhh. It doesn't sound good," Jeffrey said with a little concern.

"Oh, that. I don't think it sounds all that bad. I think I heard it when we got underway," Ian said.

Jeffrey and Ian were discussing the origin of the noise and whether it was something to worry about when Michael came into the pilothouse.

"Hey Jeffrey, I don't know if we should keep running the engine. It's way overloaded. Do you hear the snifters releasing? And the exhaust is really black."

"So you think we should shut down? We can always have Loren tow us," Jeffrey said.

"Yeah, I think we should."

Jeffrey looked disappointed.

They held a conference, and in a couple of minutes Jeffrey was on the radio with Loren. The engine was overheating, and we couldn't continue on our own. We hadn't even gotten out of Shoal Bay.

Michael disappeared back down into the engine room. The old-time sound of early twentieth century industry came to a slow end, and we were dead in the water. I went down below and found the towline we had brought with us. By the time I came back, Jeffrey had made arrangements with Loren to come alongside. I walked up to the bow with the line and handed it over to Jeffrey. Loren maneuvered the *Chief* into place and Jeffrey heaved the towline. Grant caught it on the other side.

With the *David B* under tow, Michael came back up on deck. There wasn't really anything for us to do except enjoy the ride back to Bellingham under blue skies with Mount Baker looming in the distance.

Jeffrey went down below deck to check the bilge for water. It wouldn't be unusual for a wooden boat to seep water or even have a leak. The materials between the seams are simple organic materials like cotton and oakum, and they tend to dry out and shrink when a boat isn't used. Another reason for leaks is that as the boat moves through the water, it works its planks, flexing them. It's a lot like when you stand in the middle of a bridge as a semi-truck drives across, and you feel the whole concrete structure move under your feet. As the boat moves and flexes, seams open and close just a tiny bit and water can seep in. Usually it's no big deal and the water is pumped out. It's just one of those things to get used to. Over time you learn where your boat has leaks, and you get to know how it behaves. If it changes, you note it. When you haul out, you inspect it and see if you can slow it or fix the leak, but it's common knowledge among all wooden boat owners that your boat will leak. Jeffrey was satisfied with the *David B*. Its hull was sound, and there were no big leaks.

With nothing to do but wait until we got to Bellingham, Jeffrey and Michael sat on deck planning for our arrival. Jeffrey wanted to bring the boat into its slip under its own power. Michael seemed to think that it should be all right. They speculated that the engine was overheating because the hull and the propeller were most likely covered with a thick layer of barnacles and mussels.

Not too far outside the breakwater, Michael restarted the engine and the crew on the *Chief Kwina* let loose our towline. I tried not to remind myself that Jeffrey and Michael were communicating with each other with the ring of a bell and that the steering was backward. I set up fenders and dock lines while Jeffrey and Michael practiced their bell code a couple more times. We entered the harbor. Slowly, Jeffrey steered the boat down the fairway and turned the *David B* into our new row. Ian and I held onto our fenders, ready for action. Our slip was at the far end. We crept up to it with heart-pounding slowness.

I heard Jeffrey signal twice with the bell. Michael took the engine out of gear, and when he did, the whole engine slowed down almost to a stop. I sucked in my breath, not knowing if this was normal or not.

Jeffrey lined up the *David B* for our slip, and I still held on to my breath waiting for the engine to come back up to speed. We were so close. Slowly the waltz returned to its previous meter. I breathed out.

"Ding, ding, ding." Jeffrey signaled for reverse to slow the boat's forward motion as we nosed into the slip. "Ding, ding." He signaled for neutral.

Grant and Bill had already jumped off the *Chief Kwina*, which was now moored across the dock from us. They were ready to catch lines. The *David B* entered the slip slowly. "Ding." Jeffrey rang the bell again. The engine slowed, then came back up to speed as the boat slid forward just a touch.

"Ding, ding." He signaled for neutral. I picked up the stern line and waited.

"Ding." he signaled one last time to Michael and the *David B* slowly moved to the end of the slip, its bow tight up against the rubber bumper. I handed my line to Bill. As always, a few old men had begun to gather at the end of our slip, drawn in by the hypnotic sound of the *David B's* engine. Once the boat was tied up, Jeffrey stepped out of the pilothouse, checked all the lines, then proclaimed, "Finished with engines."

I had been lying on the foredeck long enough to fall asleep, and by the time I woke up we had passed into Pryce Channel. I needed to get started on some lunch. What I really wanted to make was potato soup, but it's kind of bland and Jeffrey doesn't like it. For me, it's a comfort food and a recipe that has been passed down for at least five generations on my mom's side of the family. It's a simple soup.

You fill a pan about halfway with some water, then throw in some chopped up onions and potatoes. Bring to a boil. Next drop in a dollop of butter and some salt and pepper and let it cook until the potatoes are soft. When the potatoes are soft, pour in some milk. Bring to a high simmer. While you're waiting for the soup to simmer, make some egg noodles by mixing together, in a separate bowl, two eggs with a cup or so of flour and a dash or two of salt until you get a stiff dough. Take the dough, pinch off pieces, and drop the pieces of dough into the soup. Cook for about five minutes at a high simmer. The noodles are actually dumplings, but for five generations, the women in my family have called them noodles.

I wondered what I could do to the potato soup to make it less bland and more desirable for Jeffrey. I realized that what I was really craving were the noodles. Seafood, I thought to myself. That'll work. So I took my basic recipe for the potato soup and substituted clam stock for plain water, then added some dill and a tiny bit of cilantro along with a half cup of white wine and some scallops, shrimp, and a handful of halibut scraps I had in the freezer.

I tasted the soup. *Not bad. I wonder what Great-Grandma Brown would have thought.*

Jeffrey leaned over from the bridge. "What's for lunch?"

"Oh, you're gonna love this. I've upscaled my potato soup just for you. It's a little more like a seafood chowder. I think you'll like it a lot. I also have some bread in the oven. Lunch will be ready in about ten minutes."

"And what about an after-lunch treat?" Jeffrey asked. He's a self-avowed "treatatarian" and loves all cookies, pastries, and chips more than anything healthy or green.

"I don't know yet. I was thinking about making date squares." My sweet tooth was asleep at the time, so I had not yet come up with a treat plan.

One thing I had learned early on about Jeffrey was that he needs to be on a regular feeding schedule. It had recently dawned on me that his desire to run a passenger boat had very little to do with the romantic notion of us running a boat together as husband and wife. It was more so that he could be surrounded by good food at all times to feed his higher-than-normal metabolism. I'm not sure why Jeffrey doesn't weigh three hundred pounds, but if he doesn't eat on a schedule, he can't function properly. In our life together we talk in terms of the greater and lesser bellies. Jeffrey's is dominant and cannot be ignored, whereas mine causes less trouble and doesn't mind skipping a feeding if needed.

I was careful to plan lunch so that we could eat before we got to Yuculta and Dent rapids. I was pretty excited about going through this stretch of water.

"So this is one of the cut-off points for timid sailors," Jeffrey explained as we neared the narrows. "The book says it runs seven knots, with steep overfalls and whirlpools at max in here."

Jeffrey and Sean had both been through Yuculta and Dent rapids. Jeffrey wanted Sean to drive, so he stepped aside and watched the chart plotter while Sean steered the *David B.*

"Hey, Christine, get your binoculars out and check out that tree over there," he called out to me.

"Holy cats, there're like forty bald eagles in it. That's too cool," I said, trying to count them.

Sean steered us over toward the eagles, and then Jeffrey took the helm so Sean could join me on deck.

"That's so incredible," Sean said as he came up to the bow with his camera in hand.

"I've never seen so many in one spot and so close together. It looks like a flipp'n Christmas tree." I was thrilled. A few years ago, I had volunteered at a wildlife rehabilitation center where I worked with lots of sick and injured eagles. It was encouraging to see so many healthy birds together in the wild.

We passed through Dent rapids and the only other excitement was seeing a group of Steller sea lions hauled out on Jimmy Judd Island. Jeffrey and Sean high-fived each other. Aaron, who had been sitting in the pilothouse watching and learning how to navigate, left to go check on the engine.

★

A little while later, Aaron poked his head up through the engine room scuttle. "Hey Jeffrey, there's a lot of smoke coming from the clutch. Do you want to come down and look at it?" Aaron's voice was calm, but the look in his eyes suggested this might be serious.

"Sean, take the wheel and steer us toward the middle of the channel. Looks like we might need to shut down in a hurry. Then check the plotter to make sure that there're no rocks nearby. See what our drift is, and let me know how much time we have to before we need to start back up," Jeffrey ordered as he went below.

The steady one-two-three of the engine slowed and died. We were in the middle of Nodales Channel drifting with the current. I watched Sean calculate and then call down to Jeffrey, "The plotter says you've got fourteen minutes and thirty-seven seconds before we drift into the shore."

I went out on deck to get some fresh air. *It's a nice spot to be broken down.* The weather was calm and the sun was high. The thick forest came to the water's edge. It was silent. *At least this didn't happen a few miles back in the rapids. Lucky there's not much current here.*

I noticed a floating building in the nearby cove. I picked up my binoculars. It was what I suspected, one of many fish farms that dot British Columbia's coast. This was a nice diversion from the problems in the engine room. Through my binoculars I could see a man walking on the floats of the pens that held tightly packed Atlantic salmon. He was feeding the fish. At first, this seems like a good idea, but in reality, farmed salmon are an ecological disaster in the making. Those innocent food pellets scattered into the water contain antibiotics used to keep the penned-in Atlantic salmon "healthy." It bothers me that the food also contains dye to give the otherwise grey-colored flesh of these industrialized fish that nice pink color that wild-caught salmon attain from their natural diet. *I would never willingly serve farmed salmon,* I thought.

Sean came out on deck while I was watching the salmon farmer. I had lost track of time and forgotten we were adrift in the middle of nowhere.

"How are you holding up?" Sean interrupted my salmon meditation.

"Oh, I'm doing fine. Actually I'm surprised how 'fine' I *am* doing. I think a year or two ago, I would have been really freaked out to be adrift with a broken engine. We've had so many problems with the engine and the alternators since we left, but so far, you guys have fixed everything that has come up. I'm sure they'll get something figured out, right?" I looked over at Sean. "You know, I've used up all my adrenaline. I just don't have any more nervousness left in me."

"They say the clutch is slipping." Sean sat down on the edge of the trunk cabin.

"I wonder if they're gonna use the Bon Ami trick?" I had bought Aaron a whole case after I heard that a little sprinkle of the household cleaning powder was one of the old-timer tricks to temporarily fix a slipping clutch. "If they did that, then we could start up again and limp into a nearby anchorage to fix it." I was confident that we'd be underway again soon.

"There's a spot not too far away, but I think they're going to let things cool down a bit longer before they start back up." Sean looked around and then went into the pilothouse to watch our drift.

I'd spent enough time on deck, so I followed Sean inside. There was a lot I wanted to get done in the galley. In particular, I was excited to check on my infant sourdough starter, Whiskey Golf. I lifted the container's lid. The gooey fermenting mass was getting gross and kind of stinky. I stirred it, then took out a couple cups of glop and replaced it with a cup of flour and a cup of water. I stirred it again.

"OK, guys, keep up the good work," I said to all the millions of yeasts in the starter and closed the lid. In a week I'd be able to make my first loaf of bread.

While I babied my sourdough starter, I heard Aaron barring the engine over. Nice, they're about to start the engine. I wonder if they got it fixed, or if they'll have to work late tonight? The engine started and Jeffrey emerged. He looked around at our position and briefly talked with Sean about our choice for a close-by anchorage before putting the *David B* in gear. Aaron stayed down below to keep an eye on the temperature of the clutch. We motored about twenty minutes and dropped anchor in Thurston Bay.

It was quiet, with the exception of a few Swainson's thrushes. The water was like a polished mirror that reflected a sky checkered with small cotton-ball clouds. The land surrounding the bay had been logged maybe fifty years ago, and the second growth of spruce and hemlock was thick. There was a female common merganser with her young paddling around the mouth of a stream that flowed into the bay. Her swept-back rufous-colored head feathers gave her the rattled look of someone stuck in a wind tunnel.

With the anchor down, it was time to have a beer and talk things over. The clutch was still slipping. The guys tossed ideas around.

Jeffery got out his notepad and started drawing, while Aaron flipped through the engine's ancient manual, looking for a hint about what to do when the clutch slips.

"Hey, listen to this," Aaron said. "It says here: 'If the clutch runs hot in the go-ahead position, it is too slack and must be adjusted by loosening one of the bolts in the clutch dog collar and screwing it in about one-quarter or one-half turn.' So, fuck yeah, there you have it." Aaron closed the manual with gusto and finished his beer.

"Right, how hard can that be?" Jeffrey took the book and opened it back up to the schematic of the clutch.

"Yeah, check it out." Aaron leaned over the manual with Jeffrey.

"I love the way they wrote back in the twenties. It was so simple, direct, and flowery at the same time. If it slips, tighten it." Jeffrey picked up his beer can and took a last sip before heading down into the engine room.

It was too early to get started on dinner so I went out on deck to do some bird watching. The merganser family was still cruising along the shoreline. The mother was out in front with four or five young ones in tow. The air smelled like drying peat. Some movement by the stream caught my eye. It was big, brownish-black, and lumbering through the tall grass.

No shit! It's a bear.

"Hey guys," I shouted down into the engine room. "Do you have a moment to come up here? There's a bear on the beach. Bring binoculars."

The guys stopped what they were doing and came up on deck. They lined the port rail to watch the bear, which paid no attention to us or the boat.

"That's so cool," Sean said as the bear came into full view.

"What's it eating?" Jeffrey asked.

"I think it's eating grass," Aaron said.

"Do bears eat grass? I thought they ate salmon or garbage." Jeffrey sat down on the trunk cabin.

"I don't know, but that one seems to be eating grass," Aaron said, looking through a pair of binoculars.

"They eat grasses or sedges in the spring," I said, as I set up my scope.

"Hey look. I think he's taking a dump," Aaron said, and the three of them laughed.

"I think you're right." Jeffrey stood back up to get a better look.

The guys laughed some more, then put down their binoculars and went back to work.

The bear was a black bear, but like many black bears, this one was more cinnamon-colored, like a grizzly bear. Slowly it ambled its way around the patch of tall grass growing along the stream bank, often sitting for a few minutes at a time, munching. Time seemed to stand still as the bear dined. Other than the sweet upward spiral of the few Swainson's thrushes and the occasional buzz-by of a hummingbird, Thurston Bay was silent, and we were alone.

CHAPTER 5

THE BOAT'S DYING FASTER
THAN WE CAN SAVE IT

M/V David B -- Ship's Log					Date 6/22/06
Time	Location	Wind	Baro	Depth	Remarks
0556	Anchored Thurston Bay	30	1026	32.4	Partly Cloudy/ calm
					Clutch working Normally
1020	u/w from Thurston Bay				
2020	Anchored Pearse Island Channel			20ft	CALM
			1115	28ft	CALM

THE NEXT MORNING I stood on deck while we raised anchor. As I watched the chain slowly coming up, jellyfish floated by in the current. We needed to make almost seventy miles between Thurston Bay and the Pearse Islands. Most of the ten-hour run would be in Johnstone Strait. In general, it's best to travel Johnstone early, before the afternoon winds pick up. The forecast was for the usual small-craft advisory later in the day. The westerlies would be right on our nose at about twenty knots, with two- to four-foot seas—not a difficult task for the *David B*, but a long slog nonetheless.

The scenery was magnificent by any standard, but after the grand scenery of the days before, Johnstone Strait seemed a little mundane. The mountains along the strait are more gradual and not so high. The currents still flowed, but not as fast as at Yuculta or Dodd Narrows. Every journey and every project has the time where you work slowly toward your goal. It's the time where the end seems so far away that it's almost unattainable, and transiting Johnstone reminded me of the long years of slow work after we brought the *David B* to Bellingham. We'd begun to settle into a routine. There were times when the excitement built, just like occasional currents and whirlpools, but mostly we would be steadily punching into the continuous chop of empty open water.

Unlike the steady forward plod toward the Pearse Islands, however, once we moved the boat to Bellingham, we stopped making much progress. Without the commitment of going to Lopez Island to work on the boat, the drag of everyday life pulled us away from working on the *David B*. There were too many distractions.

We'd bought our first house. Not more than two weeks after we moved in, our homeowner's insurance company dropped us because the roof was sagging and the house needed to be painted, all work we had to do ourselves because we didn't have the means to pay a contractor.

We picked a wedding date in October of that year, and the planning filled up more of our valuable spare time. Jeffrey and I were both working full time, and I was spending one day a week volunteering at a wildlife rehabilitation center. When there was time to work on the boat, it was for only a few hours at a time. It was frustrating, and we began to lose focus.

Then, our newly laid foredeck started leaking. We had suspected this might happen because there had not been enough time to properly dry the wood we used for planking. As the planks dried and shrank, the caulking became less tight and rainwater dripped in to the fo'c'sle. It was a disappointing step backward. We were going to have to reef out all the caulking and start over. We also came to the realization that the rest of the deck was going to need to be removed, as well as all of the beam shelf, the deck beams, and the bulwarks. The stern of the boat didn't look too good, either, and Jeffrey worried aloud that we might have to rebuild the entire back end of the boat. I wondered where we would find the time and the money to do all this. The project was becoming more daunting. Everything we thought we could save turned out to be rotten.

Going down to the boat on rainy days was especially difficult. We couldn't keep up with the decay that ate away at the *David B*. The stern was rotting the fastest, and every time we stepped on board during a downpour, there was a puddle of water that collected just outside the door to the galley. Someone, a long time ago, had drilled holes through the deck and hull as deck drains. Unfortunately, the drains weren't finished correctly, and they exposed lots of end-grain wood to freshwater, which in turn created the perfect environment for rot. Another "bonus" of the deck drains was their ability to clog.

"Why can't we ever have time and money at once?" Jeffrey asked one evening. It was dark and raining, and he knelt on the deck trying to unclog the starboard deck drain with a coat hanger. "It seems like in the summer when we're making money, there's never time to work on the boat."

"And in the winter, we never seem to have any extra money to afford to do the projects that we need to do," I finished Jeffrey's sentence. "We barely have enough extra money to pay for moorage."

"We've got to stop making excuses for why we can't come down here. We're just going backward, and it's killing us and killing the boat," he said angrily, while working the coat hanger up and down.

I hate coming down here when it rains. It always makes Jeffrey so upset.

"I know, I know," I said. "I have that same fear. I worry that we're just spinning our wheels trying to get somewhere with this boat, and in the end, we'll wind up paying big bucks for someone to haul the boat, have it clam-shelled and sent off to some landfill." I wiped a drip of rain from my nose. "Every time we drive down here to check on the boat, I look out at that pretty sailboat over in the boat yard. You know the one?"

The drain gurgled and water finally streamed over the side.

"The one with the rebuilt transom?" he said as he slowly stood up. I could tell by the way he stretched out his lower back that he'd probably spent the whole day working in the *Victoria Star's* engine room.

"Yeah, that's the one. Well, I look at it every time we pass by and wonder why it was abandoned after they put all that effort into it. I heard that they ran out of money, but it seems that if they really, really wanted to finish it, they could have found the money somehow . . . right?" I looked around the *David B* and wondered about her future.

"Yeah, I hope that doesn't happen to us . . ." his voice trailed off. "But I sometimes wonder." Jeffrey walked around to the back deck and crawled through the doorless cutout in the back of the pilothouse. His red raincoat was soaked. "Let's go check the bilge."

Too many days were like this one, when we only managed to find enough time to walk down the dock to check on the boat. Every time we'd drive into the parking lot, I felt a sense of foreboding. My heart would beat bit faster as I walked toward the ramp that led to the *David B's* slip. I'd keep my eyes fixed on her mast. If it had been more than a couple of days since we'd been down to the boat, I'd hold my breath until the rest of the *David B* came into view. We had trained ourselves to look at the waterline to note exactly how far the top of the rudder stuck up out of the water. This indicated whether the bilge pump was working and everything would be just fine.

Jeffrey lifted the hatch cover in the engine room to look into the bilge. "When did the pump last run? Did you notice if it came on while I was clearing the deck drain?"

"Yeah, it pumped for ten seconds or so, but I didn't think to check the time. It couldn't have been more than a few minutes ago. Is the leak getting worse?" I squatted down next to Jeffrey for a look.

"I don't know for sure, but I think so. Look here. You can see water streaming into the bilge just behind the stuffing box." Jeffrey moved aside to let me look.

"That doesn't look so good. Will it be ok?" I asked. I was still new to the cult of wooden boats, and seeing water stream into the boat scared me.

"We'll be fine, so long as the pumps work," he said, as if the leak was no big deal.

"Do you think we need to haul out soon?" I sat back on the ceiling planking and looked at my beat-up shoes. *I need a new pair,* I thought.

"I'd like to, but there's no place in Bellingham to haul out any more, and we'd have to go to Port

Townsend. Besides, it would cost us around two thousand dollars just to take the boat out of the water, and if we're going spend that kind of money, I want to do more than just fix a leaky seam." Jeffrey leaned back next to me and looked up to watch rain dripping into the engine room.

"What can we do?" I leaned my head on to Jeffrey's wet raincoat. It was cold on my cheek.

"I've been working on a couple of ideas." He sat up. "If I can find out *exactly* where the leak is coming from, I can reach down along the hull with a can of sawdust taped to our long pike pole. Then I'll turn it over and the sawdust will float up under the boat. If the can's in the right spot, the sawdust will get pulled through the seam and help to slow it down. Who knows? Maybe it will stop it until we have the money *and* time to haul out in Port Townsend."

"Seriously? You think we can fix the leak with a can and some sawdust?" I gave Jeffrey a skeptical look.

"Oh, yeah. I've seen it done before." He smiled and his eyes sparkled.

"What if that doesn't work?" I leaned forward to look at the water in the bilge.

"Well, I guess we could call the divers and have them put a patch on the spot," he said.

"Is that expensive? What would they use?" I stood up, ready to go. We hadn't eaten dinner yet, and I was getting hungry.

"Oh, I think it would be between two hundred and three hundred dollars, so not that bad," he said. "I think they'd use a sheet of lead, some tar, and nails." Jeffrey reached for the ladder to climb out onto the deck.

"Yeah that's not too much money. I'd only have to work somewhere between twenty and thirty hours to pay for those divers. Maybe we should try the sawdust trick first. We have a surplus of that, and I'm sure we can come up with the right-sized can," I said, as I followed Jeffrey up the ladder and out into the wet night.

We walked back up the dock, leaving the boat in the rain, again. The weekend was coming soon. Maybe we'd be able to work on the boat, but the holidays were here, and it seemed that every weekend was filling up with trips to visit with family and friends.

"We've got to start spending more time down here, Christine. The boat's dying faster than we can save it." Jeffrey's head hung as he repeated what was becoming a mantra. He seemed so sad and frustrated. I grabbed onto his hand, still cold from unclogging the deck drains, and together we walked up the dock in a heavy, depressed silence.

There were so many opportunities for us give up and let the David B *die. So many days we did nothing,* I thought as we cruised through Johnstone Strait. *This boat has been the center of my life since the spring of 1998 — eight years we've spent struggling to get this boat in shape.*

Over that period of time, I'd anthropomorphized it as an old soul. When I talked to the boat in my mind, I'd ask it, *What are you thinking? Why us? How could you possibly ever have believed you could be saved by two people so financially unprepared." "Because you'll find a way,"* I imagined the *David B* would reply, and the words would float around my head before sinking to wrap themselves around my heart. Unfortunately, there had been so much work to do, and somehow we'd lost our momentum the moment that we brought the boat to Bellingham. Those first years were a letdown. We were failing the *David B.*

While I thought back on our struggles to rebuild the boat, I'd had been watching the columnar rocks on the shore and the tall trees that were growing on them. I took pleasure in the ability of the trees to make a living on the rocks, despite the poor soil they lived in and the harsh conditions they faced. As I stared out the window, I noticed that the water we were cruising through had changed from smooth to rippled.

I slid out of the settee and stepped up to the bridge deck for a look at the paper chart that hung from the overhead. It showed that we were coming up to Tyee Point and Ripple Shoal. Whirlpool symbols dotted the chart to indicate that we were entering turbulent waters. Outside the boat, the water was running quickly, like a river. In places, the surface swirled as if it were going down a drain. Then, not too far away, the water boiled back up to a smooth surface.

"Check out that whirlpool. It looks like it goes down three or four feet," Sean said to me as he pointed out one that passed to our starboard side.

"Wow. That's impressive," I said, with a little concern, and looked over to see how Jeffrey was faring at the wheel. He was smiling and clearly enjoying the challenge of steering in turbulent water. I relaxed. "Hey, check out that bigger one over there. There's a pretty good-sized log trapped in it." I motioned to the more impressive whirlpool farther away. Around and around the log spun in the whirlpool's funnel. I imagined that some giant, invisible hand was using it like a straw to stir a Volkswagen-sized Martini.

Jeffrey had begun to tell a story about maelstroms and their power when Aaron came flying up out of the engine room. "We've got to shut down right now! There's water spraying all around the engine room."

Jeffrey, Sean and I all turned to look at him with alarm. There were whirlpools outside. Unlike yesterday's emergency shutdown, if we stopped here, we'd be smashed on the rocks.

"Why? What's wrong?" Jeffrey said calmly, as he'd gotten used to Aaron needing to shut the engine down for these almost daily emergencies.

"The hose for the bilge pump has come off, and the water level in the bilge is really high, just under the floorboards. It's up to the shaft and making a huge mess."

Jeffrey thought for a moment as he wove the *David B* through the fast moving current. "I think you'll have to wait. Whirlpools trump bilge water right now, unless you can your get your arm down past the shaft safely to reconnect the hose."

"Whirlpools?" Aaron mouthed while taking a look outside.

"We'll be out of this in ten minutes or so. We can stop safely then," Jeffrey said.

Jeffrey continued his deliberate steering until we were past Tyee Point. We shut down the engine and drifted for a few minutes while Aaron reconnected the bilge pump, and then, with the daily emergency over, we headed into Current Pass.

"Hey, Christine, do you want to stick around here for a while? I want you to drive this stretch," Jeffrey said, just as I was thinking about going down to the galley to feed the sourdough starter. "Like the name suggests, there's a lot of current here in Current Pass, and I want you to know how to navigate this. There's also a lot of big ship traffic, and you'll want to pay close attention to the radio to know what's out there."

I turned to the computer for a moment and studied the chart. This part of Johnstone is divided in two by Helmcken Island, which acts as a median, like you'd see on the highway. Northbound traffic is required use Current Pass, and Race Pass is for southbound traffic. Both passes have lots of whirlpools and shoals at their ends.

"So you'll want to stay out of the middle of the channel in case a cruise ship, or something else, comes up behind you," Jeffrey cautioned me. "Right now, the only traffic I've been hearing about is a southbound cruise ship. I don't think we'll be meeting up with it until we're somewhere up by Port Neville."

We were left to our own thoughts for a while, and the only sounds in the pilothouse were the rhythm of the engine and the water rushing by outside. Jeffrey broke the silence. "Christine, do you think you're ready to drive on your own for a while? I need a nap."

'Sure," I said and asked Sean if he'd stay on the bridge in case I had any questions.

Despite the fact that I had owned this boat for eight years, I really didn't have much experience boating. It seemed that there was never any time for us to enjoy being on the water.

One of the few times we had taken the boat out during the rebuild was for a time trial in the bay. We needed to know how far we could make it in a day so that we could plan our trips. The test course was a measured mile printed on the chart and delineated by some markers on shore.

We still didn't have any controls for the engine in the pilothouse, so Jeffrey asked Grant, who had been on the *Chief Kwina* on the day we brought the *David B* to Bellingham, if he could drive while Jeffrey operated the engine down below. A few other people came along for the evening cruise.

To make it more difficult, the bell and jinglers that we had used previously for bridge-to-engine room communications were no longer aboard. They belonged to a friend of Jeremy's, and he had taken them back after our first voyage.

"So, here's the plan," Jeffrey explained as we prepared to get underway. "I'll be in the engine room, and Grant's going to be on the bridge. Christine, I need you to stand at the back of the pilothouse near the opening to the engine room. Grant's going to shout to you, and you are going to yell down to me whether I need to shift the boat into forward or reverse. Does that sound all right to you guys?"

"Roger that," Grant confirmed.

With the engine started and the lines off, Grant stuck his head out of the pilothouse and said, "Reverse."

I repeated his order: "Reverse." Then I cupped my hands around my mouth and shouted "Reverse!" to Jeffrey, who stuck the long metal bar into the clutch and shifted the boat into reverse. The boat moved backward.

In a moment, it was time for "forward." Same thing. Grant told me "forward." I repeated "forward," and then shouted "forward" to Jeffrey, who put the engine in the ahead position.

We made it out of the slip and were cruising down the aisle with the "ching, ching, ching . . . ching-ching ching" of the engine. We needed to make one left turn to exit the harbor. We nosed out of our row and Grant started the turn. The *David B* swung wide, and I could see that we were going to be awfully close to the boathouses on the other side. I stood there waiting for Grant's next command, wondering if our homeowners' insurance would cover us if we crashed through the nearing boathouse. We didn't have any insurance for the *David B*.

"Reverse," Grant said, sticking his head out the pilothouse door. He looked calm.

'Reverse!" I shouted down to Jeffrey.

The boat continued going forward, with the corrugated-sided boathouse looming closer. I heard

Jeffrey shift the engine, but the *David B* is heavy, and her momentum continued. I knew there was an expensive boat in there. I wanted to close my eyes.

"Can he give me some more?" Grant said with a slight bit more urgency.

"More reverse!" I shouted back down to the engine room. But I heard nothing.

"Jeffrey! More!" I shouted louder.

Five feet separated us from the boathouse, now four feet. In my welling panic, I couldn't think of the words I needed to tell Jeffrey to slow us down. I screamed down into the engine room, "More faster backwards!" This time he heard me, and the engine throttled up. I looked ahead toward the boathouse; we were now less than a foot away.

"Oh, shit." I breathed in. Despite still wanting to close my eyes, I kept them open.

We had begun to slow, but it was too late. The stem of the *David B* glanced down the side of the boathouse, leaving a 10-foot long black mark and a minor dent in the corrugated metal. Inside the boathouse, the dock moved with the impact, but the boat inside was safe. My head pounded with relief.

"Forward." Grant stuck his head out of the pilothouse, looking a little shaken but relieved that he'd gotten just enough reverse from Jeffrey to keep from really hitting the boathouse.

"Forward!" I repeated into the engine room, feeling the tight muscles in my face relax.

I stayed at my post until we cleared the breakwater, then let Jeffrey know we were out of the harbor and done shifting.

"More faster backwards, huh?" Grant cocked his eyebrow up at me as I stepped up into the pilothouse.

"It just sort of came out," I said, a little embarrassed that I'd panicked and couldn't think of the right words when Jeffrey didn't respond. I looked back toward the harbor as Jeffrey emerged from the engine room.

"Thanks, Grant. That worked out great." Jeffrey said, smiling as he joined us, apparently unaware that anything had gone wrong.

"Well Captain, it seems that the *David B* turns a little wider than I was expecting," Grant explained.

"Yeah, I start my turns a lot sooner than I think I need to," Jeffrey said.

"We left a pretty good skid mark down the side of the boathouse back there." Grant stepped aside so that Jeffrey could take the wheel.

"We did what?" Jeffrey said with a puzzled look on his face.

"We hit the boathouse after I tried to get you to go faster in reverse, but you didn't hear me." I gave Jeffrey my version on the story.

"Is everything ok back there? I didn't feel anything." Jeffrey was suddenly concerned about what he had missed while in the engine room.

"Nothing was damaged," Grant said.

"I was wondering why you needed so much reverse back there." Jeffrey shrugged off the incident. "I guess we should go do some time trials."

138

This stretch of Johnstone Strait was long, wide, and deep, and, after the fun of Tyee Point and Current Pass, it didn't involve any difficult navigation. It was a good place for me to drive. Sean stayed on the bridge deck, but we didn't talk much. He was engrossed in making some whippings for the dock lines. Although I was a bit nervous—this was more or less my first real wheel watch—I enjoyed the experience. Being at the wheel felt good, like I was a part of the boat, and remembering the incident with the boathouse made me realize how far I had come in my maritime education. I asked Sean a few questions about boat handling, and he answered them while he sewed.

My view out the pilothouse windows included Johnstone Strait and the bow of the boat. The raised trunk cabin on the main deck was shiny with varnish, and the mahogany skylight that Sean had made a couple months earlier looked beautiful in the center of the cabin top. It was a piece of artwork that would always be part of the *David B*. The fir decking still glowed like new. I tried to recall what it had looked like just before we started taking the old tarred deck off. It had taken years to finish the deck, and the details ran together in my mind. I tried to sort through all the steps and the people who had helped.

In the fall of 2000, my grandparents gave us some money. It was enough to build a good-sized shop, with some money left over for the winter—an exciting opportunity for us, since it meant that Jeffrey could work full-time on the boat for a couple of months. I had also changed to a slightly higher-paying job. We felt like things were going in the right direction for us. One day, Jeffrey came home from running errands really excited to have run into an old neighbor of ours.

"Hey, do you remember Tom, who used to live next door to us on Wilson Street? I ran into him at Hardware Sales today. Do you recall how he was taking that Westlawn class? Well, he finished the naval architecture program and is now living out on San Juan Island and looking for work. He wants to come by some time to see what we've done," Jeffrey said.

"That would be great. I'd like to see him again. When is he planning to stop by?" I asked.

"I don't know, but seeing him gave me an idea I wanted to run past you." Jeffrey paused. "What if we asked Tom to come and work for us this winter? I think if there were two of us, we could get a lot more done."

I thought for a while. It wasn't what I was expecting. Without Jeffrey's income, we were already going to burn though the money from my grandparents in three or four months, and if we hired Tom, that meant that we'd blow though it a lot faster. On the other hand, with Tom working for us, Jeffrey *could* get a lot more done on the boat. I figured we'd probably have to take out a cash advance on a credit card to pay Tom, but it might be worth it if it meant we could make real progress.

"How long do you want him to work for us?" I tried to think of all the consequences. "Do you think it's worth the expense? I worry about going into debt to pay him. You're already taking the whole winter off to work on the boat. As it is, you're not going to get paid until you go back to work on the *Victoria Star* in April."

"I really think it'll be worth the risk. It's not like we're borrowing to buy a new TV or skis or something. It's money we're investing in the *David B's* future. If Tom agrees to come and work for us, we'd be getting 80 hours a week of labor in between the two of us. I think we could get the whole deck finished. We'd really make a difference," Jeffrey lobbied.

I sighed. "You really think this is a good idea? I don't know. I like the idea a lot. Tom's a good guy and he'd do good work, but I just worry about not being able to pay our bills in February or March. Let me think about if for a while."

A couple weeks later, Tom pulled up outside our house. It had been several years since I'd seen him. He looked the same: medium build with short dark hair. He'd packed his bucket of tools in the trunk of his car. Tom had agreed to spend a couple of months working with Jeffrey. Since he lived on San Juan Island, he would take the ferry each week and stay at our house for four days at a time.

I had a regular job, so I didn't get to help much on the *David B* that fall. In the evenings, I would come home from work and start a fire in the fireplace and make dinner. As I pulled ingredients out of the fridge and cupboards, I looked forward to Jeffrey and Tom's arrival. I loved hearing about the work they were doing, and I was jealous of how much fun they were having being constructive while I had to go to my dull job as a receptionist. It was nice that the job paid more than Soundings of the Planet, but staying put at a desk from eight a.m. to five p.m. had begun to make me feel more like I was in prison. Every morning as I turned onto the road to International Market Access, two ominous yellow road signs greeted me: NO OUTLET and DEAD END. Their message was grim. Every morning, I talked back to the signs, telling them that I had a plan and that I would escape my dead-end job.

As the kitchen filled with the smells of garlic and onions, I'd forget about my job, and soon Jeffrey and Tom would come walking through the door, laughing about some part of the day. They'd decided that Tom had become a mule, hauling innumerable cartloads of rotten wood up the dock, and that Jeffrey was tuned into the schedule of the garbage-truck driver so that the moment the dumpster was empty, they would fill it back up again with rotten *David B* deck and bulwarks. The evenings around the dinner table, with mounds of pasta and a roaring fire, made me feel like I was still part of the project. Here I could be included in the planning and the laying out of ideas for the days and weeks ahead.

It took almost a month for Tom and Jeffrey to remove the main deck, and during that time Jeffrey obsessed about the best way to redo it. As often happened, he formulated a plan while we were running.

"Since our brand-new, traditionally laid foredeck leaks like a frick'n sieve, let's not do that again." He took a breath. Then he asked, as we ran down our alley in the early morning darkness, "I was thinking about using plywood. What do you think?"

We always start our runs a little fast; Jeffrey's a jackrabbit and I'm a tortoise.

Breathing hard, I replied, "I don't know . . . what's the . . . advantage of plywood? Is it used . . . for boat building?"

"The advantage is that we can make it completely watertight. The last thing we want to explain to passengers is that the deck leaks are part of traditional seafaring. Having water dripping on your forehead in the middle of the night won't be acceptable as an authentic experience." Jeffrey half laughed as we turned the corner.

"Doesn't plywood . . . come unglued . . . when it gets wet?" I panted.

"No, there's marine plywood that has special glue," Jeffrey said.

I grunted a bit to let Jeffrey know I had heard him and that the pace he set was too fast. We ran in silence for a while.

A tight deck would make our future passengers happy, I thought. *But does Jeffrey really know what he's doing? I'll wait for the next downhill to ask.*

"It's perfectly normal to build a deck out of plywood. I can show you some down in the harbor." Jeffrey practically sang as we headed up a short hill. It was still dark, and the crushed limestone trail glowed just enough for us to see our path.

Jeffrey had tricked me into the sport of running when he bought me a pair of running shoes and told me they made me look sexy. I'd only been running for a couple of years, and hills of any length were still a struggle. "Nah . . . if you think you . . . know what you're . . . doing, then . . . I . . . don't need to go on . . . a special field trip." We crested the hill and the trail flattened out. I could breathe easier. "How will we keep the seams from leaking?"

"We can fiberglass them—and by the way, good job on that hill back there," he said.

"Thanks," I said, before asking, "How would we finish the deck? Do we paint the plywood or put that rubber coating like on the *Chief Kwina* or *Phoenix?*"

"I don't know yet. I'd like the deck to look traditional, but I'm not yet sure how to do that. Maybe we could make some planking that's not as thick as the planking on the foredeck and glue or screw it down to the plywood. I think it would look a lot better," he said.

We finished our morning run. It was just beginning to get light outside. I was happy that Jeffrey had figured out what to do about the deck. In the back of my mind, I worried that the leaking foredeck was my fault. I hadn't totally understood that the purpose of giving one side of each plank a slight angle was to make a half v-shaped seam for the caulking. I feared that I had made the angled edges too wide on most of the planks I'd done, and that had made the seams hard to caulk. Then, as the green wood shrank, the seams widened more, causing an even leakier deck. If it was my fault, Jeffrey has never said.

We were still a long way from being able to lay decking down. As it was, there were a number of other problems to solve. One night at dinner, Jeffrey started discussing his plan for the beam shelf. "My idea is that we take some two-by-fours and epoxy them into place. We need to build it out to thirty inches."

"Are we going to try to glue and clamp the whole thing at once?" Tom asked.

"No, I was thinking we could nail each of the successive two-by-fours to the previous one and then, once the shelf was as wide as we wanted it, we could drill through the entire shelf, hull and guard, and then drive a rod through the hole." Jeffrey took a piece of paper and began diagramming.

"Are you going to go through the frames?" Tom scooted his chair in closer.

"Good question. I think we might need to go between them, because I don't want to run into the fasteners that are already there." He leaned back so we could see the diagram.

With the plan in place, Jeffrey went on a buying spree. The receipts piled on my desk faster than I could deal with them. Wood, plywood, fasteners, epoxy, drift rods, augers, nuts, and washers were all expensive. I tried to ignore how fast we were going through our winter's nest egg as I prepared myself for the eventuality of having to use credit cards to pay for the rebuild.

It's ok. We're investing in the boat. As soon as we're done with the rebuild, the boat will start to make money and we'll be able to pay off our debt, I repeated to myself over and over when I started to worry about our one-way cash flow.

Tom's last day was a few days before Christmas. Jeffrey had overestimated how much work they could do. While they hadn't laid the decking, they had actually gotten a lot done. I stood on one of the deck beams and surveyed all the new wood that was painted with primer. The beam shelf was complete on both sides of the boat, and all the deck beams were in place. In the middle of the boat, Tom and Jeffrey had built the sides for the trunk cabin and the frames for the cabin top. It felt so good to look at our dream coming true.

A southbound cruise ship approached as we neared Port Neville. It was a big boat and would have a big wake. A few people on its deck took pictures of the *David B*, their automatic flashes going off like distant firecrackers. I looked around the galley to see what might fall over when the wake got to us. I didn't want some crashing dish to wake up Aaron or Jeffrey, who were still sacked out on the settee. As the wake arrived, I turned the *David B* into it and we rode comfortably over the tall swells. Jeffrey stirred and opened his eyes. "Huh?" he said through the cloudiness of sleep.

"Cruise-ship wake," I told him.

"Right." He lay back down and was once again out cold.

The cruise ship industry is so efficient. It's funny to be left here bobbing in their wake. I gripped the wheel with a mix of anger and jealousy. *They have so much. So much money for advertising. So many options to convince people that their cruises are the only way to see Alaska.* We were sinking deeper into debt with each day that the phone didn't ring. I wondered if the people snapping pictures of the *David B* would rather have gone cruising with us if only they had known we existed. *I hate money.* I leaned into the last succession of smaller waves that passed under the boat. *It's the only thing that's keeping us from making this life work.* I straightened us back out on to our course and made a wish, for a single day of Celebrity's advertising budget.

I shifted my stance at the wheel. I was tired of standing and reached behind me for a stool to sit on. We had a long way to go yet. The wind was kicking up, and the waves were choppy, but the *David B* sliced through them. As I looked out at the endless waves that marched down Johnstone Strait, each wave reminded me of a moment in time and how easily it slips by.

We fell still further behind with the rebuild in the winter of 2001, and the *David B* languished. Our lives changed. We got new jobs. Jeffrey had become bored with his job as a ferry boat captain. A friend helped get him a job with Western Towboat, taking barges to and from Alaska. It was our hope that he could have big blocks of time off when he could be at home, working on the boat. The pay and the benefits were also better than anything he'd had before.

My commute past the two road signs proclaiming NO OUTLET and DEAD END had finally gotten the best of me, so I took a summer job on a whale-watching boat. I had gone from making twelve dollars an hour to seven-fifty. The pay cut was hard, but it gave me a few months of soul searching. In that time I discovered that variation, movement, creativity, and independence were the qualities that mattered most to me in a job, and those ideals guided me in my quest for a new career.

When my summer of contemplation was over, Garden Rescue was born. It was my first business and was immediately successful. Even though I started it in the fall, the usually mild climate kept me busy into the winter. I gardened every day for eight to ten hours and dropped the twenty pounds of weight I'd gathered by sitting at a desk. I was physically exhausted but the happiest I'd ever been at work. Most of my clients were cat ladies and widowed men. They all loved their yards. It was an honor for me to work in their gardens. Often times I would weed with my clients, doing the work they no longer could, and we'd talk about family and life. I tried working commercial properties, but they felt like empty, soulless wastelands of Mugo pine, English ivy, and cigarette butts. I avoided them.

That must have been 2001. The same year that Jeffrey started working for Western Tow Boat . . . That's when I almost sank the boat. I closed my eyes with sadness at the thought.

I missed Jeffrey's company. He had been gone for a week, heading to Whittier, Alaska, on a towboat. If the weather cooperated, he'd be home in another week. We were both having our doubts about the towboat job. It seemed that Jeffrey was gone more than he was home. It also seemed that as soon as he was ready to get a few days of work done on the *David B*, the dispatcher would call and ask if he was available for work the next day or sooner. Not wanting to turn down work, Jeffrey would leave and be gone for two to three weeks at a time, our plans set aside for later.

The consequence of our new working lives was neglect of the *David B*. We tried our best to get work done in the small amounts of free time we had. This time, before he left on the towboat, Jeffrey had asked me to varnish the new fir on the inside of the trunk cabin.

I was up to four coats when the temperatures dipped and the snow came. I woke up in the morning and saw several inches of my favorite form of precipitation. *Snow holiday!* This meant that I could cancel my gardening appointments, start a fire, make a pot of coffee, scramble up some eggs, and clean the house. Outside, the wind was blowing and snow swirled around the house, making drifts in the yard. I wished Jeffrey were home and we could be warm and cozy together.

The snow and cold wind lasted for several days. *I really should go down to the boat and check on it,* I thought more than once, but then I'd look outside and decide it could wait until the next day when the roads would be better or the wind would die down. I wasn't worried about snow load on the boat, because we had built a big white plastic cover over the *David B.* I loved the cover. It kept the wind and rain out of the boat, and because people couldn't see us working, it also kept the curious from stopping by and slowing down our labor with questions, kudos, or skepticism. The cover was stout, and Jeffrey built it for the eventuality of snow.

After a week of procrastination, I finally got up the motivation and drove to the harbor. I pulled into the parking lot. The boat was still there. I could easily see its mast. I got out of the car and started walking to the ramp, looking at the boat the whole time. The big plastic cover was still there and had made it through the winds. That was good. I walked down the ramp. I looked at the waterline of the boat. It seemed different. *The boat's riding way lower in the water* seeped into my mind. I was too far away to tell for sure. My heart knew something was really wrong, but my brain kept up the denial.

No, that's how the boat always sits in the water. You've just forgotten what it looks like. My heart raced and my feet sped up. I kept looking at the boat as I walked, knowing it was different and dreading what I would find.

It's okay, it's the same, quit your worrying. My denial kept me company up to the moment I got to the boat. I paused at the stem and looked for the scum line, that little indicator of where the boat usually floats was underwater. I knew the boat was taking on water. My mind raced as I walked to the door of the cover. I unlocked it. I lifted the door open and stepped in, onto the nearest deck beam. Inside, I held on to the pilothouse door for support. I closed my eyes to clear my mind and prepare for what I would see. I wanted to keep them closed as long as possible, because I didn't want to see how much water was inside the boat. *Oh, B boat, I hope I haven't let you down,* I thought. I told my panicked heart, *If it's bad, just get the emergency pump and pump it out. Once it's dry, call Jeffrey. It's not going to be all that bad.* I felt a wash of calm with the small plan I had developed.

Ready? I opened my eyes and looked down between the beams.

"Oh, shit, shit, shit," I said as the momentary calm flew out the door. *Fuck, where's the pump? Shit, Loren has it and his boat isn't in its slip. Holy crap. I've got to find Loren.*

The water was not where I was expecting it. It was higher. A lot higher. The floorboards were floating and moved gently with the motion of the boat as I moved around on the deck beams. The pump I needed was supposed to be on board, but we'd recently loaned it to Loren. I fumbled for my phone. My hands were shaking and my heart was pounding.

I scrolled through my contacts, looking for Loren's phone number. I found it and dialed. It rang, and it rang, and it rang. I tried to control my breathing. Voice mail. Too tongue-tied to leave a message, I hung up.

I stared at the phone, trying to think about who to call next. Drew, Jeffrey's former boss, would know what to do. I dialed Victoria San Juan Cruises and the longtime office guy, Sean, answered.

"Hi Sean. Is Drew around?" I asked trying my best to sound normal.

"Oh hey, Christine. No he's in Palm Springs this week. He'll be back Monday. Do you want me to let him know you called?"

"No I just had a question for him. How about Grant? Is he there?" I was thinking fast. It felt good just to talk with someone. My panic was subsiding since the water level was not rising visibly. I had time.

"No, he's working at George's today," Sean said.

"Thanks, I'll give him a call. You don't happen to know where Loren is, do you?" I asked.

"No, is something up?" Sean questioned me.

"No not really, I just need to find our big pump and Loren was the last one to have it. Thanks, Sean." I hung up and started looking for Grant's number. I found it. I dialed. I tapped my right foot nervously as I waited for the ringing to start. The phone rang a couple of times and Grant answered.

"Hi, Christine," I could hear a little bit of surprise that I was calling. Usually Jeffrey calls Grant.

"Hi, Grant. Do you know where Loren is? His boat's not here and I need to find him. He has our pump and the *David B* is . . . The *David B* has . . . There's some . . . There's a little water. There's some water in the boat." I tried to control the words coming out of my mouth, but I couldn't get them out right. I stammered and stuttered, and my voice shook.

"Uh, roger," Grant said slowly, as if he was trying to fully understand the mess of words that had flooded out of my mouth.

"So, you are looking for Loren to find your pump?" he repeated calmly.

'Yeah, that's right," I said. "We loaned him our pump for his trip over to Port Townsend, and we never thought to get it back."

"Roger, and you have water coming in?" Grant asked.

"Yeah, it's way up over the floorboards in the engine room."

In the background, I could hear George's voice asking what was going on. Grant repeated what I had just said. I could hear George. "Oh, Jeffrey's boat's sinking?"

My mind screamed. *Oh, God, he just said the S-word!* I felt the rush of tingling panic return to my body. It was like a strike of lightning. I realized that for the last few minutes, I had been so careful not to use the S-word. Hearing George say "sinking" made my skin and muscles feel prickly and my hands sweat.

"I think Loren had the *Chief* at the sawtooth," Grant continued.

"The sawtooth?" I asked. A serene, clear calm came over me. The sawtooth is a dock just at the other end of the harbor. I could simply walk over there and get Loren and the pump. "Great, thanks Grant. I'll see if I can find him."

"Okay, give me a call back when you get everything under control. You might also try stopping by the port office. They should have a pump you can use," Grant said.

"Good to know. I'll try them last. I'd rather the port didn't know about this. Thanks for your help, Grant."

I stared for a moment at the water in the engine room and decided to call Jeffrey. I knew that I should wait until the ordeal was over, but I wanted his help and I wished he were here. I dialed and got his voice mail.

"Hi Jeffrey. I'm trying to find Loren. There's a lot of water in the boat. It's up to the floorboards in the engine room. Loren still has our pump, right? Anyhow, I'm sorry to call you. I know there's nothing you can do while you're out on a tugboat, but I'm kind of freaked out. I just called Grant and he said Loren was at the sawtooth. I'm going to head over there next. Call me. It will be all right." I hung up and stared some more at the water. The level had not really changed. I still had time to find Loren and get our pump without letting the port know that we were sinking at the dock.

My phone rang. I looked down at the screen, it was Loren.

"Hi Loren," I said.

"Yeah, Christine, Grant just called. What's this about your boat sinking?

Damn, there's that word again.

"Well, I just came down here to check on it and there's a bunch of water. It's up over the floorboards.

I'm not sure what happened, but do you still have our pump?"

"Yeah, Christine, I sure do. Can you hold tight for a few minutes? I'll be right over with it."

"I sure can. I'll see you in a few." I was once again left with my rotten old and now sinking boat.

Shit. Why the fuck didn't I get off my lazy fat ass and get down here sooner? I leaned my head against the pilothouse. *I'm so sorry B boat. I shouldn't have neglected you. I promise, I'll never put you off again. Please forgive me.*

I wondered what went wrong with the bilge pumps. *Had the power had been out? Maybe the water level had risen past the pumps and shorted them.* I didn't really know, and I didn't much care at this point. *I just want the water out and the pumps working.* I was mad at myself for not checking on the boat, and I was irrationally mad at Jeffrey for being gone, even though he was working a job that he disliked.

When Loren arrived, I felt relived. The boat would be rescued from its slow sinking at the dock. He had our big heavy pump in a dock cart, and alongside it was its long plastic three-inch-diameter suction hose.

"Hi, Loren. Thank you so much. I'm so embarrassed."

"Not to worry, Christine, Let's have a look and see what's going on down there," Loren said as he stepped on board. "Yup, it sure looks like you've got some water in the boat. It's not that bad. I've seen a lot worse. We'll get you fixed up here in no time at all."

With that, he connected the hose to the pump, and I took the suction end of the hose and fed it down to the lowest part of the engine room.

On the dock, Loren primed the pump and pulled the cord. The loud lawn mower-like engine came rumbling to life. The pump gushed water in a wide and continuous stream. The water level fell rapidly. I wanted to cry but decided I could hold back until Loren left.

It took less than five minutes to empty the boat of its unwanted water. When it was dry, Loren went to work to see why the bilge pumps had failed.

"We've got two pumps." I climbed down into the engine room to show Loren where they were. "One's under the shaft, and the other's in the middle of the boat."

Loren rooted around in the bilge at the back of the engine and produced a pump. There was still a little water in the very deepest part of the bilge. He played around with it for a little while I watched.

"This one seems to be fine. I'm not sure what happened. Maybe the power was out," he said and we walked up forward to the other pump. After a little more rooting around, he found it.

"Well, here's part of your problem. It looks like the wiring has come undone," he said after a minute of looking at the pump.

One little pump gone awry and my lack of attention almost cost us the boat. I looked around at the scum left on the inside of the boat's ceiling planking.

"Well Christine, I think you're good to go," Loren proclaimed after fixing the wire.

"Thank you so much, Loren. We owe you big. I can take care of the pump and its hose unless you still need it on the *Chief*," I said.

'No Christine, I don't need it. I'd been intending to drop it back by for a long time," he said.

"Well, I'm glad you had it. Otherwise I'd have had to do this all on my own, and it felt better having you help. I wouldn't have known what to do with the wire."

"Well, all right, then, I'd better get back to my boat. Let me know if you need anything else." He climbed up the ladder and then ducked out the door.

We had once again dodged a major bullet. I looked around at the boat. It was a mess. Where the water had been, there was scum. The whole boat was dingy. All the new primer was stained, and it depressed me. I stayed for a while and cried. I promised the boat that I'd never skip a day of checking on it.

I felt better after a while, and with my new promise to the boat, I got up to leave. As I was locking up, the automatic bilge pump turned on for a few seconds. I was happy to see it working again. I paused for a moment with my hand on the lock, looking down at the water.

I left the boat and walked up the dock. The wet snow was melting and made slushy footprints behind me. When I got to the top of the ramp, I turned back toward the boat. *I'm sorry B boat. I'll see you in the morning . . . I promise.*

An alarm startled me. It was Aaron's. Time to check the engine. Jeffrey was awake now too, but stayed lying on the settee, staring at the ceiling.

"What's for dinner?" Jeffrey asked.

"I don't know. I was thinking about making pasta. You ready for the wheel now?"

"Yeah, sure. Is there anything I need to know about?" He stepped up to the bridge deck.

"Nope, there's no traffic. We've got about an hour to the Pearse Islands." I gave Jeffrey the wheel.

My first real watch on the *David B* was done. I'd even begun to feel comfortable at the wheel. It really boosted my confidence, because I had done it on my own, even though Sean had been there as my coach.

I was in the galley prepping for dinner when Jeffrey shouted, "Porpoises! I think they're heading our way to ride the bow."

We grabbed our cameras and ran to watch.

Their presence was the highlight of an otherwise long and mostly uneventful day. The porpoises were like that good friend who agrees to run the last miles of a marathon with you. As they played in front of the boat, they would occasionally turn on their sides to look up at us, as if to say, "Job, well done. You're almost there. Just another mile to go. You can do it."

As we came to the entrance of the Pearse Islands, the porpoises left us. Our marathon day in Johnstone Strait was done and I was looking forward to dropping the anchor. We'd only experienced one problem, and I hoped that was a good sign. Tomorrow was a big day and another test of the *David B* and its crew: We were going to cross Cape Caution.

"That's an awful lot of salad." Sean laughed as Aaron leaned over the railing to look at the anchor, which was hanging at the waterline. Its flukes were backward, pointing toward the hull of the boat. The current was flowing rapidly, and Jeffrey was already at the helm with the boat in gear to take us out of the Pearse Islands' narrow western entrance. Aaron and Sean would have to right the anchor while we were underway.

"This blows," Aaron said, annoyed that the anchor had come up the wrong way.

To flop the flukes away from the hull, he needed to remove the mound of seaweed that had accumulated on the anchor and obscured the spot where he wanted to insert the pike pole. Aaron reached down with the pole and pulled out as much seaweed as possible. His inner six-year-old couldn't help but throw some seaweed at Sean.

"Kelp!" Sean laughed while deflecting a long chunk of seaweed.

Aaron again took the pike pole and stuck it down behind the anchor to try to pry it upright. Sean kneeled by the windlass, ready to release the brake and clutch to finish raising the anchor.

With the anchor in place, Aaron went down to the engine room to speed up the Washington. He came back up after we were sure everything was working right.

"You've always got a smile when you come up the ladder. What are you thinking?" Sean asked Aaron.

"Don't know." Aaron smiled back.

It was true; Aaron always has a smile when he emerges from the engine room. It could be he's thinking about the bag of chips he's going to dive into, or some joke he's telling himself. Probably it's the fact that he's going to get to start napping again.

"Hey, guys, look over there." Jeffrey pointed toward the shore on Cormorant Island. It was early, about 0630, and the water was glassy calm. There was a spray followed by the emergence of a tall black fin. A lone male orca whale was slowly cruising the shoreline, his six-foot tall dorsal fin knifing through the still water.

"What a great way to start the day," I said, grabbing the binoculars. There were a couple boats out, with a few fishermen in them. They may have noticed the whale but seemed too interested in their fishing to care about the whale.

This orca was less than a quarter mile off our port side, and we paralleled him for a while. We didn't go out of our way to watch him, but were happy to see him nonetheless. He was going a little faster than our six and a half knots and eventually, he passed us. At some point, he dove down, and we never saw where he surfaced.

"Let's double-check that everything is tied down. The forecast is for six- to eight-foot swells, and they're going to be on our beam, so we'll probably get rolled around a little," Jeffrey said. "Once we pass Cape Caution and make the turn, it shouldn't be too bad, but I don't want dishes falling out of cabinets. Sean, can you make sure everything on deck is secure? Aaron, you've got the engine room, and Christine, you've got the galley. Since we don't have latches on the cabinets yet, you'll want to tape them shut. It'll be about 1300 before we start feeling anything."

We would be leaving the protection of Vancouver Island that we had been enjoying for the last few days. Today we would get to feel the Pacific Ocean. It was once again a great day and we were beginning to feel very lucky; high pressure had been following us up the coast, and we'd been having unusually beautiful weather.

I'd been quietly worried about crossing Queen Charlotte Sound and passing Cape Caution. This bit of the Pacific made me anxious. My mind filled itself full of images of rogue waves with angry monster combers bent on destroying the *David B.*

You're just afraid of the unknown. Look at Jeffrey and Sean. Are they afraid? To check my growing and irrational fears of Cape Caution, I watched Sean and Jeffrey's body language. Sean had recently sailed on the *Lady Washington* for a trip to the Caribbean and enjoyed ocean waves, and Jeffrey had crossed Cape Caution numerous times working for Western Towboat; he was excited that today's forecast predicted a low, comfortable swell. For days, he had been carefully watching the weather. A change might have prevented us from crossing for a day or even longer.

As I secured the galley, I had decided that sandwiches would be a good lunch and got ready to make some bread. My plan for the rest of the day, until we rounded the cape and got back into protected water, was to hang out in the settee with my binoculars, watch birds, read a book, knit, and nap. I'd probably get to drive for a while, but there really wasn't much to do except enjoy the feeling of the boat and the warm sun as it shone through windows.

The gateway to the open water is a cluster of tiny uninhabitable islands called the Jeanette Islands. Pacific rollers dash their weather-beaten rocks. The windswept trees give warning that you are crossing through to another level. Beyond them, we had six hours on the open ocean before we could relax behind the protection of Calvert Island on the other side.

On the surface of the swells were numerous birds: rhinoceros auklets, common murres, pigeon guillemots, and marbled murrelets. They were all oblivious to what I perceived as the hazards of Cape Caution. I watched the birds to keep my mind busy. Occasionally a bait ball would form, with hundreds of gulls and seabirds clustered around a school of fish. They dove, swooped, and gobbled in a frenzy, all of them squawking and calling with excitement. Then the fish would escape, and the frenzy would end suddenly. A cluster of birds would mark the spot where the bait ball had been, until the cry of a gull would begin a mad dash to the next ball of fish.

As the waves slowly intensified, I watched the galley for movement. Things were doing all right. I was comfortable as the boat rolled with the rhythm of the ocean.

"Hey Christine, we're going to be getting a few bigger ones in a moment," Jeffrey said, and with that the boat rolled a little harder, sending stools across the galley floor and the door to the engine room scuttle opening and slamming shut. Jeffrey gave me a "get on it" look and I scurried around, looking for a spot to stow the stools, and taped the door shut.

"I think you'll want to put hooks and latches for the stools and scuttle down on the to-do list, huh?" Sean suggested.

Once everything was secure, I went up to the bridge deck to hang out for a while and to take my turn driving. Before Jeffrey asked me to take the wheel, I held on to the windowsill and watched as we rose on the swell and descended into the trough. It's an unsettling feeling to be surrounded by water, and while the swells we were in were benign, the ocean has subtle ways of reminding you of its infinite power. As we rhythmically rode through the waves, I thought about our good luck. Several times, I caught the splash of humpback whales breaching in the distance. We had been granted a perfect day. Jeffrey stood aside and taught me how to steer the boat in the larger waves. As I'd feel the boat rise up over the top of one wave and then descend into the trough, I'd correct the steering a spoke or two at a time. At the horizon, the sea and sky met to blend into the same color of blue. Occasionally a sea bird would draw my attention, but mostly I focused on the feel of the boat as my confidence in myself and the boat grew.

"What's it say?" Jeffrey asked.

It was mid-November 2004, and we were sitting in the parking lot of Bellingham's downtown post office.

"It says 'the Port now requires all boats to have insurance,'" I read aloud from the letter I had just opened. "I think we're screwed."

We sat silently in the car for a few moments, the windshield wipers intermittently wiping away the raindrops that fell like the tears gathering in my own eyes. I tried not to show emotion, but I feared this was the end for the *David B.*

Jeffrey exhaled, then backed out of the parking stall and drove us home. We didn't talk. There wasn't anything to say. We just wondered what we were going to do about the *David B.*

I read through the letter from the port once more, then left it on our table. Despite the rain, we had planned to drive to the Fragrance Lake trailhead to go for a run. It was supposed to be a fun afternoon, but the letter from the port changed the mood. I didn't want to go any more. I just wanted to sit on the couch and stare at the wall.

I felt numb as I reluctantly put on my running clothes. *Why does everything have to be so difficult? We just had a good day of working on the boat, and now this.*

Jeffrey drove us to the trailhead. I watched him the whole, way trying to read his mind. The muscles in his jaw flexed and pulsed, and his eyes focused down the road. When we pulled into the parking lot, it was raining hard. It promised to be a muddy run, and I looked forward to stomping in some puddles to lift my spirits.

The first few steps were cold, and I tucked my hands up into the sleeves of my jacket. It was late afternoon and we had a little more than an hour of daylight left. I felt stiff and unsure of myself. This trail was always difficult—uphill for two miles. At first I just listened to my breath and the sound of our feet.

"You know, we've always known we were taking a risk by not insuring the boat," Jeffrey began.

"Yeah, I know," I said as we moved through the gate that keeps mountain bikes and horses off the trail.

"It just never made any sense for us to insure the boat," he said as we started up the first switchback. "It would have cost more money for us to insure it than we've spent fixing it, and in its current state, I'm not even sure we could *get* insurance."

"I know. We've talked about that a lot. You always say that if you can afford to lose something, then you don't need to insure it, and we've always been able to afford to lose the boat. In some ways we'd probably be better off if we just gave up on it," I said before the trail got too steep for me to keep up my end of the conversation.

"What do you think we should do, then?" Jeffrey asked. He was a few paces behind me.

"Don't know," I grunted. He'd have to wait until the trail leveled off before I could give him his answer, which was nice because it gave me time to collect my thoughts.

I watched the trail for roots and felt the diffused rain dripping through the canopy of Douglas fir, Western red cedar and Western hemlocks. It was drier under the huge trees, but still the rain fell. The sound of raindrops on sword ferns and salal in the underbrush lulled me into deeper thought, as did the rich smell of moss and sweet humus of decaying leaf litter.

What do we do? Shit, I don't know. What are our choices? Can we even get insurance? Who would be willing to insure our piece-of-crap boat?

"Did you see that the old boatyard is reopening?" Jeffrey interrupted my thoughts.

"Yeah, I did. Do you think they'll have a large enough TraveLift to pick up the David B*?"*

"From what I heard, it sounds like they will. The newsletter in our last moorage bill said that they'll be open in a couple weeks . . . You know, we're going to have to haul the boat one way or another."

The trail leveled out a bit as we went past my favorite trees, three young cedars perched atop a boulder. Their graceful roots drape off the rock and into the soft soil below. I call them The Muses.

My legs were tired from the switchbacks, so I waited until I felt recovered to answer, "What do you mean, 'one way or another?'"

"We'll have to haul out the boat either to have a survey done so we can get insurance or to have it destroyed. When big old wood boats like ours are too rotten to save, they break them up with excavators and chainsaws and haul them to the dump. It's the only way to get rid of them. It's not very pretty seeing one get the clamshell."

"I guess you're right. Maybe it makes sense to at least *try* to get insurance before we decide to demolish it."

"Yeah, that's kind of what I was thinking," Jeffrey said, then asked, "Do you mind if I run ahead for a bit? I'll wait for you at that next junction."

"That'll be fine. I need some time to think," I replied and moved aside. Jeffrey sped up and I lost sight of him as he rounded a corner.

Maybe this whole boat idea was just a dumb dream that we're wasting our time on. The David B *is just too far gone. No one is going to insure it. Maybe I should be happy that the port sent us that letter.*

I worked my way up the trail to meet Jeffrey. It felt good to be running. It soothed my anxiety. When I got to the junction, we ran the rest of the way together. It was still steep, so I didn't talk much. Jeffrey asked a few questions about the upcoming Thanksgiving dinner we were going to be hosting. I answered when I could, but mostly, I just kept going, one step at a time.

Thanksgiving didn't seem that important compared to this new struggle with the boat.

A few days later, when Jeffrey scheduled the haul-out, I realized the gravity of our situation. I was driving across town when he called to let me know. After I hung up, I just kept driving. I felt like I needed to escape. My palms on the steering wheel began to sweat. Outside forces were pushing us to move faster than we could afford, and I wanted to run away from our struggle. As I drove without direction, I thought, and I worried.

How are we going to have time? And where's the money going to come from? He doesn't realize just how much this is going to cost us. Jeffrey's ideas are always so glass-half-full. We're already struggling with moorage, and now we're going to have to add the cost of having the boat in the shipyard. I came to a stoplight and looked at my hands. My knuckles were white as I gripped the wheel. *We lost the security of a good paycheck when Jeffrey quit Western Towboat and began to work with me.* The light turned green.

Maybe, just maybe, the answer is for Jeffrey to work full-time on the David B. I'm sure I can work more hours, or hire more employees so that the gardening business might be enough to support us both. My anxiety faded, and I searched for a parking lot to pull into. *The faster we can get out of the shipyard, the better off we'll be. If we can save the boat, then we can start marketing our trips. Even better, if we can get passengers lined up, then the boat can start paying for itself.* I had no idea just how much this thought was actually going to cost.

I pulled into the first parking lot I saw and sat in the truck for a few moments, pondering the haul-out. I felt strangely giddy that Jeffrey could save the boat if he just had the time and we had the backing of passengers. I loved the boat so much, and I felt that a surveyor would agree that it could be saved. I got my phone back out and sent Jeffrey a text:

> may b u should
> work full time
> on the b

The scheduled date of the haul-out was December 4. We also contracted with a ship's surveyor who had extensive experience with wooden boats to do an initial survey. If he thought we could still save the boat, we would ask him to help us outline what we needed to do. I liked that we had a plan.

When Jeffrey's parents and Aaron's family arrived for Thanksgiving, I felt confident that I was prepared to talk about our new plan. Our Thanksgiving was a potluck, with Jeffrey's mom, Ann, bringing my favorite pumpkin pie and Aaron's parents, Jack and Barbee, surprising us with some side dishes. We had wanted to cook something different than the normal turkey dinner, so I had found a recipe for a stuffed pork tenderloin with pistachios and dried apricots. We had also invited several other friends. As they arrived, the house was filled with the delicious smells from the oven. Soon the kitchen was overcrowded with cooks and bystanders.

While we cooked, Jack poured me a glass of wine, his booming voice rising over the other conversations and kitchen noise. We talked about the *David B.* He had been one of our most positive supporters, especially after a sailing vacation we had gone on together a couple of years earlier. During that trip, he had recognized our talent and encouraged us to follow our dream.

"Well, I think that's it: dinner's ready," I announced, as I took Jack's green beans out to the table. We all found seats and began to pass dishes around.

"To good friends." Jack raised his glass. "Our two families have been sharing our holiday meals for almost thirty years. It's wonderful that we are today passing the tradition off on to the next generation. To both of our families, and to Jeffrey and Christine."

We proposed a couple of additional toasts and began to eat. As dinner went on, I could hear part of a conversation that Jeffrey, Jack and Aaron were having at the other end of the table.

"What do you think the surveyor is going to say after you haul out?" Jack asked.

"I think the only major thing we are going to need to do is rebuild the transom and put in a few new frames. The rest is cosmetic at this point; sand the hull and paint it. The deck is finished, with the exception of laying down some fir to make it look nice. I'm sure if we could get the transom rebuilt, we wouldn't have any issue getting insurance. The rest of the boat is sound," Jeffrey replied as he reached for a second helping of mashed yams.

"About how much do you think that will cost, and how long will you need to spend in the shipyard?"

"Right now, my best guess is thirty to forty thousand if we do all the work ourselves. There's no way that we afford to pay the labor costs for someone else to do it. I think we could be done by spring."

"That sounds reasonable. What's your plan to finance the costs of the haul-out and the materials?" Jack asked and then poured himself some wine before passing the bottle around.

"Christine and I have been talking about that a lot," Jeffrey said with a smile. "I think we have enough equity in our house. Up until this point, we've tried our best do work on the boat with cash we have and not go too far into debt to rebuild it. I think we've realized the only way to start up this business is to use whatever credit we have, and a second mortgage on the house should take us about halfway there. I think we're going to have to use one or two of our credit cards. It's not what I want to do, but we can't get a bank loan."

"Have you tried the Small Business Administration?"

"Yeah, we looked into that, but we don't qualify. We're too risky, and the banks that would be making the loans just don't know who we are and what we're capable of. The business bankers are still being super conservative, even though the home lenders will give a loan to any old warm body."

I was trying to have a conversation about gardening with Ann, but Jack and Jeffrey's discussion at the far end of the table kept distracting me. I wondered what people were thinking about our situation. I poured some more wine and took another helping of the stuffed tenderloin.

"So, then, how long do you think it would take for you to be up and running as a business once you're out of the shipyard? Is there some risk of a Hidden Fuck Factor? Do you know what shape the hull is in below the waterline?" Jack sat back in his chair.

"Ha, that's funny." Jeffrey laughed and smiled. "I guess there's always a chance of a Hidden Fuck Factor. I suppose there could be a plank or two that we would have to replace, but the boat's pretty tight, except for that one spot in the back of the boat."

"And how long after the transom gets fixed before you could carry passengers?"

"I think it would take six to eight months to put in all the electrical, plumbing, and cabins if we could somehow work full time on the boat, but I think in reality, it might take two years." Jeffrey stood up. "Anybody else want something from the fridge while I'm up?"

Jeffrey walked past me and gave my shoulder a reassuring squeeze before getting another round of beers.

"So Jeffrey . . . and Christine . . ." Jack turned to me to get my attention. "Aaron and I have been talking about your situation since you called a couple of weeks ago, and we were wondering what your thoughts are on having Aaron work with you to finish up the boat."

"How so?" Jeffrey asked, looking a little surprised.

"Well, he'd buy into the boat with the money he inherited from his grandfather. It would cover the shipyard expenses, and he'd help you work on the boat," Jack proposed.

There was silence at the table. I looked at Jack, then Aaron, then Jeffrey. Someone's chair scooted on the hardwood floor. Then it was quiet again. I was too shocked to say anything. *His money and his skills would really help us. With Aaron, we might make it.*

"I've done a lot of construction work on custom homes since I moved to Leavenworth," Aaron added, breaking the silence.

"Didn't you just get a job up at Stevens Pass working a chairlift?" Jeffrey said with renewed enthusiasm. "Would you keep that job?"

"He can probably do both," Jack answered.

"My schedule is set so I have three days a week off, but it hasn't snowed much. I should have been working today, but the ski area is still on standby, waiting for the snow to fly."

"So you could stay here and work when you weren't at Stevens," Jeffrey confirmed.

"Yeah, that's right," Aaron said. "I won't be able to be here for the haul-out because of some training I have, but I could start the following week."

Holy cats, I thought, trying to keep a straight face. *Did he just offer up his inheritance to buy into the boat?*

"So when we *do* get the boat up and running, would you want to sail with us?" Jeffrey asked. "You could be the engineer. You've worked on marine engines before, and the time you spent in the motorcycle shop would translate to running the Washington."

"Yeah, that's exactly what I was thinking." Aaron tipped back his beer, then leaned in on the table, a newly minted crew member of the *David B.*

We changed course. We had been heading west across Queen Charlotte Sound and had just reached Cape Caution. *Halfway there*, I thought, as I looked at the spray from waves crashing on the rugged shoreline by the light structure that marked Cape Caution. The new course meant that we would have a more comfortable ride in a following sea toward Fitz Hugh Sound.

I had carefully scheduled a full day of garden work for the date the *David B* was to be hauled. I was simply too nervous to watch. Our friends Lisa and Dan helped Jeffrey take the boat to the shipyard. I'd given my camera to Lisa to take pictures of the boat as it came out.

While I anxiously weeded and raked, across town, one of my fears had come true: the yard had refused to haul out the boat. Jeffrey sat in their office like a school kid called into the principal's office. Outside, the *David B* floated like a fish caught in a net. Its hull rested against a set of loose slings, waiting to be brought out of its marine world and onto dry land. It was about to be the second boat lifted by the new lift, but when the owner of the shipyard saw the decrepit *David B*, he put a stop to the operation.

"I'm worried about two things," the owner told Jeffrey. "First, your boat is kind of rough, so I'm going to have to use all of my slings to lift it. Even then, I'm not sure we won't crush your boat's frames, and I'm not about to be responsible for that.

"Second," he explained to Jeffrey, "I don't want to end up owning the boat if you don't finish the project. More than once we've seen dreamers like you start a project, then abandon it in one of my yards."

He gave Jeffrey three months. "If things aren't progressing, I'm gonna dispose of that boat and send you the bill. And," he added, "I'm going have you sign on your contract that you know all this."

Jeffrey agreed to his terms, and the owner agreed to haul the boat. We still didn't know if we were going to be able to save it, and there was a good chance that we would spend the next three months chain-sawing up the *David B* and hauling it away to the landfill.

Slowly and carefully, the TraveLift operator raised the *David B* out of the water, and along with it came an entire reef of mussels and barnacles. Years worth. As the *David B* hung in the slings, water dripped from its hull. The last time the boat was hauled out was 1981. It had been careened on the beach a couple of times to have its bottom scraped, but that was all.

My cell phone rang. It was Jeffrey. "Is the boat out of the water?" I asked without even saying hello.

"Yes. What time will you be here? I'm going to need the truck," he said.

"I've got about an hour or so more gardening to do. How does it look? Did it go all right?"

"It looks good, but they were not very keen on hauling us. They almost wouldn't do it. I had to sign a contract that they can destroy the boat if we don't look like we're doing anything."

I breathed in, "Really? It was that bad?"

"No, they just want to cover their bases," he said.

"What does the bottom look like?" I asked.

"Uh, I don't know yet. There's an underwater garden of sea life I'm scraping off, but the boat held up well. Nothing appeared to collapse. I'm pretty optimistic that the hull's in good shape."

"Well, that's good. I'll finish up here and be over to see it soon," I said.

"Oh, if you have anything in the back of the truck, you'll want to empty it out. It's going to save us a couple hundred dollars if we remove and dispose of the mussels and barnacles ourselves."

"Hmmm. I guess I'll be a little later, then."

I hung up the phone with a sense of foreboding. The boat made it out of the water—just barely—but not only was there a chance we couldn't get insurance, now the shipyard also had the power to pull the rug out from underneath us.

I had to remind myself to relax. When I got to the gate, I could see the *David B*, still hanging in the slings, with its keel no more than a foot above the ground. The boat was so much bigger out of the water. It was still dripping from its pressure-wash bath. Jeffrey was busy scraping mussels off the boat. There were thousands of them, and the air smelled like a fish market.

"Did all these come from the *David B*?" I asked, leaning out the window of the truck's cab.

"Yeah, I've spent a couple hours cleaning up the hull. The good news is that the planks in the water are all good and strong. I don't think we'll be replacing anything from the pilothouse forward."

"Well, that's good." I hopped out of the truck.

"Do you have both grain scoops with you?" he asked.

"I do. I guess that means these all are going in the truck, and we need to get to the dump before they close, huh?" I climbed into the bed of the truck to get the scoops.

'You guessed it. And by the way, your camera's in the car. You should go get it and look through the pictures that Lisa took," Jeffrey said, taking a grain scoop from my hand.

I set my scoop against the truck and walked across the yard. I stopped halfway. It was too big to look at up close. I felt a twinge of panic. *This is real. It's going to change my life.*

I looked through the pictures of the boat being hauled out of the water. *I can see why they were reluctant to lift it*, I thought as I scrolled through the photos. *The boat looks like a piece of shit. If it were me, I wouldn't have hauled it.* The *David B*'s stern was rotten, and the bow didn't look much better. There were no bulwarks, and Jeffrey had recently filled in some seams with Portland cement. He was only partway through sanding and painting when we got the port's letter, so the topsides had a sloppy calico look to them. The billboards that protected the hull from the anchor were rotten and popping off. The overall look of the *David B* was like that of a nearly dead salmon coming home to spawn.

I picked up my grain scoop and joined Jeffrey in shoveling mussels into the back of the truck. The pile was huge. As we scooped we listened to the sound of mussel shells popping and clicking; a few gulls came by for a free meal.

It took us an hour to load the truck and get to the dump. As we rumbled up to the scales, the office girl stepped out and said, "Back again?"

"Yeah," I said, "but this time it's garbage, not yard waste."

I backed the truck into the shed where big machinery was moving an enormous pile of trash. We opened up the plywood doors to the truck's bed and began to shovel out the mussels.

"Where'd you *get* that?" a worker asked as if we had somehow found treasure.

"It came off a boat," Jeffrey said.

"Wow, that's a lot. Too bad you can't eat 'em," he said staring at the mussels. You could almost see that he was thinking about taking a few home to cook for himself.

"Yeah, maybe cooked in a little beer and garlic," Jeffrey said, throwing another scoop out the back of the truck.

"So, what's your guess as to how much this weighs?" Jeffrey asked while he closed the doors.

"I don't know. How about seven hundred pounds," I guessed.

"I bet it's more than that. I'm gonna guess twelve hundred pounds."

"Seriously? Do you think?" I looked at him.

"Well, think about it. A garden shovel is calibrated to lift approximately eight pounds so that a man working all day won't tire. We were using grain scoops that probably hold fifteen to twenty pounds of mussels per scoop. If we each did forty scoops, that would be twelve hundred pounds, and I'm sure we've done that much, maybe more," Jeffrey said.

"I guess we'll find out." I started up the truck and headed back to the scales to be weighed again.

The girl in the office handed me the receipt, and Jeffrey eagerly scanned it for the weight.

"Nineteen hundred sixty two pounds!" he exclaimed. "Wow, that's a ton! And that pretty much maxed out our truck."

"Well, that explains why it handled so smoothly," I said and we pulled out of the dump and headed home.

With the Cape behind us, Jeffrey scanned the rocks up ahead and renewed his deep appreciation for the ease of GPS. He loves paper charts and always has two posted in the overhead. One shows the big picture of the area and the other shows a close-up view with more details.

"Those rocks all look alike, and somewhere up there is Barry Rock. It's a shallow rock and we should see the water washing over it. We want to keep it on our port side and go in with that unnamed island, one to the left of Bilton Island, on our starboard," Jeffrey said, scanning the line up of imposing rocks.

The rocks and small islands were lined up like football players, and it felt a little like we were going to crash into their defense. If we could get past Barry Rock, we'd be in.

"I *love* GPS. Look at that track. Without this, you all would be up on deck doing bow watch, and I'd be back here freaking out that we'd smack right into Barry Rock," Jeffrey said.

"Yeah, didn't one of George Vancouver's boats ground out here somewhere?" I asked.

"Oh, I think they went aground just about everywhere," Jeffrey said.

"That must have sucked, being out here with all that shit to hit," Aaron said.

"How are we doing over there, Sean?" Jeffrey asked as Sean leaned toward the computer screen.

"Looking good, sir," Sean answered.

"So who do you think Barry was?" Aaron asked.

"Someone who had a bad day once, huh?" Sean answered.

'Yeah, you really don't want a rock named after you. It's bad enough to go aground, but to have your name on a chart marking your fuck-up forever's really got to hurt," Jeffrey said.

"No shit," Aaron said.

As we went past Barry Rock, the islands absorbed the swell. Instead of feeling like an imposing barrier, they felt like loving guardians. We had entered Klaquaek Channel, where the water was flat, and the scenery had changed from clean Zen-like open water that spilled emptiness on forever to a busy maze-like jumble of islands, rocks, and coves left by the sloppy construction of ancient glaciers. We had returned to the cul-de-sacs and avenues of the Inside Passage. Here, branches hung low to the water and kissed the surface. Dead trees stood alongside living ones, their silver bark shining in the sun. We turned into Fry Pan Bay and anchored.

"The sun's still up and I think we all deserve an end-of-the-day beer on deck," Jeffrey said and headed to the cooler as Aaron shut down the engine.

The air was still, and it was hot out. It felt like summer should. There were no other boats nearby.

"The *David B* rode those waves so well. I'm really impressed with the ride," Jeffrey said, proud of his boat. It was the first big test of our workmanship and the *David B*.

"Are you nervous about the survey?" I asked Jeffrey the day after the boat was hauled.

"No, I'm not worried. The hull's in better shape than I thought it was going to be. I don't think we have anything to worry about, and I don't think he's going to tell us the boat's too far gone. I hope he doesn't say that, anyway." Jeffrey smiled as he helped me get ready for work.

"Really? You think so?" I said, crawling up onto the front bumper of the truck to check the oil and steering fluid. I wasn't as convinced.

"Yeah, this is good. Dave's going to show up this morning and spend half the day digging around the boat with his knife, sticking it into all of the planks to look for soft wood, and I'm going to follow him around and ask lots of questions. I've already been through the boat, so I think I know where most of the problems are." Jeffrey checked my hedger and blower for fuel, then loaded them into the truck. "Since I already know we're going to have to rebuild the stern, I'm going to pick his brain about it. He'll be able to tell us what steps to take. It's all good."

"I'm glad *you're* so confident. It makes me feel better," I said before getting into the truck to head out for work. My stomach fluttered as I drove off.

I stopped by the boat at lunch. I could see Jeffrey as I crossed the yard. He was standing at the back of the boat, just staring up at the stern. His shoulders were slumped. He didn't see me, and as I approached, I watched him take out his knife and begin stabbing at the planks overhead. I could see rotten wood falling to the ground. My heart sank.

"Why so glum?" Jeffrey smiled. His baseball cap was peppered in a sprinkling of wood so rotten it looked like bark mulch. "He didn't tell me to cut it up or anything like that. Actually, he was encouraging. He was pretty realistic about it, too. He said he could see from what we've done that we could probably finish it, but it's going to be a lot of work."

"Really? The surveyor thinks this is something we can do?" This was such a relief. "I've been so sad all morning, thinking that Dave would find something fatally wrong with the boat and we'd have to have it crushed." I gave Jeffrey a big hug. "So tell me how it went. What did he do, what's our plan, and *more important*, what's for lunch?"

While we celebrated over pizza, Jeffrey explained how Dave had crawled all through the boat with his hammer and pocketknife, tapping with his hammer and listening for the sound of rotten wood. When the tap would thud, he'd gently stab at the wood, checking to see how bad the rot was. Jeffrey said that he made lots of notes and took a few pictures, and that the two of them had talked for a long time about Jeffrey's ideas on how to rebuild the stern, which Dave agreed was in sad shape. By the time Dave left, Jeffrey had a clear picture of what needed to be done. He also said that Dave would send us a report with more details in a week.

"So, it looks like we're ready to go big," Jeffrey proclaimed. "As soon as we finish lunch, we should start moving tools down to the boat and order plastic for a new house that we'll have to build over the back of the boat so we can work under cover. I should probably call Greg to see how soon he can start, and Aaron, too. I heard on the news that Stevens Pass still isn't open yet. Maybe Aaron would like to move in until it snows."

Once Jeffrey has an idea, the plans often come really quickly. He was the most animated I had ever seen him. I wondered whether before he felt this new confidence he, too, had been just as worried about the fate of the boat as I had.

CHAPTER 6

THE SWAINSON'S THRUSHES
BEGAN TO SING

M/V David B -- Ship's Log

Time	Location	Wind	Baro	Depth	Date 6/24 Remarks
0240	Fry Pan Bay	Calm	10/2	45.4	Clear and
0840	U/W FROM FRY PAN BAY				outside of dock
0900	NORTH PASSAGE FROM KLAQUAET SOUND				
1700	SECURE SHEARWATER				

WE LEFT FRY PAN BAY by a different route than we had entered, through an enticingly narrow passage to the northeast. It was about fifty feet wide, with a small islet off our starboard side and a submerged rock near the exit. It's the type of close-quarters navigation that Jeffrey enjoys. He steered around the hazards while Sean called out directions based on the information from the GPS. With his newfound appreciation of its accuracy, Jeffrey felt as if a whole new world had been opened up to him. There were so many more places that he was willing to go.

The *David B* passed the rock. Jeffrey quickly made a sharp left hand-turn followed by a sweeping right, and we again headed north, this time in Fitz Hugh Sound.

A few days after the haul-out, Jeffrey met with our friend Greg, a thin, wiry guy on a beer and Yamchilada diet. Jeffrey wanted Greg to remove and then reconstruct a section of the back of the boat called the "rim log" or the "horseshoe"—essentially the large timbers that curve around the back end of the boat and tie it all together.

All of the wood back there was rotten, and we joked that the only thing holding the boat together was habit. Jeffrey had also found evidence that it had been rebuilt once before, maybe while the boat was still in Bristol Bay, but whatever might have happened to the *David B* was lost long ago to history.

We sat around our dining room table, and I listened to their conversation. Jeffrey went through page after page of scrap paper, drawing diagrams. Over the course of the evening, we consumed most of a half-rack of beer. I headed to bed before Greg left and fell asleep to the muted sound of their voices through the wall. In the morning, when I got up to make coffee, I found amongst the empties a collection of drawings in one neat stack, suggesting that Jeffrey and Greg had a plan.

About the same time that we hired Greg to help out with the rim log, Aaron came to live with us. It was a good test of how we would work together as a crew in close quarters, since we live in a small 1930s two-bedroom house that's about 800 square feet. The house is perfect for two people but a little crowded with three.

With Aaron, Greg, and Jeffrey working full-time on the boat, progress really picked up, as did the number of empty beer bottles in our recycling bin. The house was a mess, with wood chips everywhere: in our car, on the floor, on our chairs and couch, in the bathroom and kitchen, and—more often than not—in bed with us. No matter how much we seemed to clean, sawdust became a steady part of our lives.

During the days, the guys worked nonstop on the boat. In the late afternoons, I'd come to the boat to clean and paint. At night they made plans for the next day while I made meals.

Every day was like Christmas, with the UPS truck driver making a steady stream of deliveries. There was always somebody coming or going between the shop and the boat. Jeffrey and I started getting up at five a.m. to work on a new website for marketing the upcoming trips to Alaska. We'd work at our desks until eight, when Aaron would get up and the real workday would start. The busy chaos of boat restoration was delicious, and both Jeffrey and I thrived as the *David B* moved toward rebirth.

"Shearwater Marina Harbormaster, this is the *David B*," Jeffrey said over the radio.

"Go ahead, *David B*," the voice crackled.

"I'm looking for overnight moorage for a 65-foot boat. Do you have anything available?" Jeffrey asked.

"*David B*, can you stand by for a moment?"

"Roger, standing by," Jeffrey said. Sean was scanning the dock with binoculars, looking to see if we would have a place to tie up.

"*David B*, Shearwater Harbormaster. Looks like I've got a space on the outside at the end for you. Will that be for just one night?"

'Uh, roger, just for one night," Jeffrey repeated.

"Roger, one night."

"Starboard side tie," Jeffrey said, and we all sprang into action.

Jeffrey moved the *David B* closer to the dock. Aaron had the spring line in his hand and was ready to jump from the boat. A mixed collection of men stood and watched, some from a tugboat, some from yachts. All were mesmerized by the engine as it sang its siren song. Aaron tried his best to ignore them. All he wanted was to be tied to the dock and drinking a beer. These guys were going to be a distraction, and he really didn't want to start up a conversation.

He jumped and walked to the spot where Jeffrey indicated he wanted the line to be tied.

"Spring's on," he shouted, and Jeffrey put the boat in gear to pull in the stern. Aaron walked to the bow and caught the bowline while giving one-word answers to the spectators. Then he escaped the old-guy crowd by heading to the engine room to shut the engine down. Aaron's departure didn't faze them. They just moved on to Jeffrey and Sean to get their answers.

All of us were excited to be tied to a dock for the night. We'd been traveling for just over a week. The last time we'd been off the boat was in Nanaimo, and we were ready to go ashore to celebrate our accomplishments like true sailors. We'd made it halfway up the British Columbia coast. We'd crossed Queen Charlotte Sound without incident, and we'd been able to keep the *David B* running despite all the daily problems. We needed a few drinks. A couple rounds of pool, some shuffleboard, and some really bad karaoke made Shearwater the perfect port for a celebration.

Jeffrey, Sean and I were up around 0700 the next morning. I sat in the back of the settee massaging my forehead and slowly drinking coffee while we discussed what needed to be done before we left Shearwater. Jeffrey's list included filling the water tanks and buying some engine oil. Mine included fresh veggies and beer. We also wanted to get out and explore ashore before we got back underway.

We left a note for Aaron, who would no doubt sleep in as long as possible, and walked up the dock. Not too far from the top of the ramp, there was a Laundromat, and behind it we found a steep dirt road that curved around and out of sight, leading to who knows where. We trudged up it. Sean and I took pictures of old machinery and quaint gardens while Jeffrey talked about ideas he had on how to improve the boat.

At the top of the hill, we discovered a carved driftwood sign that read SPIRIT WALK and pointed toward a narrow path through the muskeg. We looked around to see if it was a public trail, then decided to follow it. The ground under our feet was soft and squishy. Where it was too boggy, there were planks to walk on. Cotton grass dotted the meadow-like muskeg as if it were miniature Truffula trees from Dr. Seuss's imagination. Throughout the muskeg there were stunted and shore pines, each one not much taller than five feet. All kinds of specialized plants make their home in this environment. The most interesting to me was the tiny carnivorous sundew; its pink and orange color and sticky glistening leaves set a deadly trap for unsuspecting insects. We followed the walk into a young forest. The ground was firmer, and the dense trees offered shade and a stark contrast to the open muskeg. As we entered the forest, the peaty smell gave way to the clean scent of spruce, and we talked about the change. The walk was short, only about twenty minutes or so, but the experience felt mentally cleansing. With our spirits lifted, we headed down the road and back to the boat.

Later that afternoon, and with Shearwater far behind us, I walked out to the back deck to check the temperature of the chest freezer that Jeffrey had converted into a refrigerator. He hadn't had time to install a fan, and the eggs kept freezing. As I stepped up onto the back deck, I felt a rush of joy pulse through my body. *I can't believe we're actually here. It seems like it*

was only a couple of months ago when we thought that we were going to have to destroy the boat, and now here we are cruising to Alaska. I stopped to watch the fizzy trail of water our wake left behind and took in the beauty of Finlayson Channel while I recalled the days shortly after the *David B* was hauled out of the water in December of 2004.

Jeffrey and Aaron began their work in the shipyard by building a shrink-wrap plastic structure to cover the back twenty feet of the boat. When they finished, it looked as if the *David B* had backed into an enormous marshmallow. The spacious cover gave us a place to work that was out of the wind, rain, and occasional snow. Once the cover was in place, Jeffrey hung several sets of florescent lights, and we were ready to begin the real work of rebuilding the *David B.*

Jeffrey and I were both excited to get started. In addition to the surveyor, Jeffrey had also consulted with several other wooden boat builders about his plan for removing the horseshoe and rebuilding it. He was worried about maintaining the shape of the boat and wanted to remove as little as possible at any given time.

On the first day of the demolition, I finished gardening in midafternoon and couldn't wait to get down to the boat to see how much work had been done. As I walked up to the cover, I could hear Jeffrey, Aaron, and Greg laughing between the sounds of the Sawzall and ripping wood. I stepped into the cover. The whole space had the damp smell of fungus and sawdust. Jeffrey was happy to see me and hurried me up on deck.

"What do you think?" he said as I climbed up the ladder.

"Wow!" I scanned the area that used to be the back deck. They had removed the plywood and were in the process of removing the deck beams. "Do you think we'll be able to reuse those beams? It would be a bummer to have to throw them away since we just installed them a couple of years ago."

"Oh yeah, we'll be able to use them again. Having to remove them is our punishment for building on top of rotten wood. I was thinking we could just store them on the foredeck until we're ready to put them back," Jeffrey said.

"That's good," I said, relieved that we weren't going to be wasting good wood.

"You should come over here and have a look at the rim log."

I stepped across the beams to the port side of the boat where Greg was working. He had a hammer in hand and clawed away at the big timbers that had been slowly decaying over the years. The rim log, which we casually called the "horseshoe," was the big U-shaped timber that held the back of the boat together. It was made up of four or five large pieces that had been scarfed and bolted together. The outside was rounded, while the inside had straight edges. To strengthen it, the inside corners were reinforced with large triangular braces. The bolts that held the braces to the horseshoe were easily several feet long.

Greg picked up the Sawzall and carefully positioned its blade between the bottom of a deck beam and the top of the horseshoe to cut through the fasteners. As I took out my camera, Jeffrey handed me a set of hearing protectors. "Safety first," he said with a grin.

I snapped as many pictures as possible so we would have a record of what was there originally, in case we needed a reference. Greg finished his cuts and removed the deck beams. The horseshoe was now fully exposed. Jeffrey came over to see what it looked like.

"Look at how they just cut each piece out of a single log, and there's no heart center. I wonder how big *those* trees were." Jeffrey kneeled down to inspect the seventy-four-year-old workmanship before taking the first stab at its removal.

I put my camera back in my pocket and climbed down the ladder. Jeffrey and Greg started throwing rotten wood overboard. On impact with the pavement below, the rot-blackened Douglas fir made heavy wet squishing sounds. Between tosses, I shoveled the earthy remnants of the rim log into garbage cans. What had at one time been strong wood had turned to soil.

When everything had been removed and my landscape truck filled, I went back up on deck to take more pictures. I felt somewhat unnerved as I looked at the unconnected plank ends that reached out into empty space. They seemed so vulnerable and delicate without the stout horseshoe and deck beams to fasten to. I could see why Jeffrey had taken the time to carefully prop up the stern with jack stands and six-by-sixes.

Several days later, and with the old wood gone, Greg got started bending long, thin strips of wood around the back of the boat that would serve as the bottom layer of the new horseshoe. At the same time, Jeffrey and Aaron began the process of making new frames. As with everything Jeffrey does, he had spent a long time thinking about how he was going to get new frames into the boat.

"So . . ." Jeffrey said with a long pause, allowing me to stop what I was doing and pay attention. "I've got a new idea for how to do the frames."

"Oh yeah? What?" I looked up.

"Ok, so here's the problem. Most of frames are in between the outside planking and the inside ceiling planking, right?"

I nodded, thinking how funny it was that on boats, the interior ceiling planking ran up the sides of the boat and not overhead.

"We're not going to remove the ceiling planking to put the new frames in. Originally, the frames were steam-bent into place or cut out of a single piece of wood to give the boat its shape. We can't slide in a sawn frame between the planking, and steam-bending isn't practical because of the cost of good oak." He stopped talking for a moment to make sure I was following along.

"Are you thinking about that technique that uses plastic frames that Loren or someone was telling us about a couple months ago?"

"No, my idea is to laminate the frames into place. We'll buy a bunch of fir and run it through the bandsaw to re-saw it into quarter-inch-thick slices. The frames we have now are three inches thick, so we can glue together twelve slices and then slide them down the frame bay between the existing frames. The best part is that while the glue is wet, the frame will be flexible and will bend itself into shape as we drive it down. What do you think about that?"

"It sounds great, but how will you drive the frames into place? Will you hammer them or somehow use a come-along?"

"Oh, I think the frames will slide in easily. We should be able to tap the new frames into place," he said.

Over the next few weeks, Jeffrey and Aaron developed a routine of making and installing frames. Aaron did most of the band sawing in the mornings, and when he had several frames worth of quarter-inch slices, he'd load up his Toyota pickup truck and meet Jeffrey down at the boat. When they were ready, Aaron would fill a container with epoxy glue and enough filler to make the glue the constituency of peanut butter. He'd slather each slice of wood with epoxy and then carry the bundle up the ladder. Then the two of them would work together to install the frame. With more than a hundred frames to do, we went through seemingly endless five-gallon containers of epoxy and bales of filler—which was not cheap.

The first few frames were easy. They were short and could be set in place. It was when Jeffrey and Aaron had to guide them between the hull planking and the ceiling planking that things got tough. The notion that we could simply tap the frames with a sledgehammer turned out to be wrong. They often fanned out or split and sometimes refused to slide down the frame bay. It proved to be difficult and tiresome.

"Could you use a come-along?" I asked one morning as we headed out for our usual running loop around the neighborhood.

"A come-along. That's a good idea, but how would we attach the wire?

"Really? You think so?" I had made countless suggestions about things to do on the boat, almost all of which had been turned down. "I hadn't thought past the come-along. You really think it might work?"

"Yeah, it's a great idea. We just need to come up with a way to attach the wire," Jeffrey said. We ran down the dark streets for a while longer, and by the time we got home, Jeffrey had come up with a new plan for the frames. It seemed simple enough: He'd drill a hole through all the slices of wood, an inch or so from the end, and he'd make a short metal strap that he would put between the middle two slices. A special counter-sunk nut and bolt would hold everything together. He'd attach the come-along's wire to a strap and winch the frame into place from inside the boat near the keel. Aaron and I both liked the idea—Aaron probably more, since he'd been doing most of the banging on the frames.

The come-along worked well. Jeffrey mounted it to a board so that it was more stable to use. While Aaron glued frame slices together, Jeffrey cleaned out each frame bay with a modified chimney sweep's brush and a vacuum. He pulled the wire of the come-along up the frame bay. Aaron attached the strap from the top and guided the frame as Jeffrey pulled it into place. It was fast and efficient.

When they were done pulling, each frame stuck up two feet out of the deck. The last step was to clamp the top to a guide so that it was in exact alignment. The frame ends remained exposed and became the stanchions that would later be topped with a stout timber called the rail cap. As the frames went in one by one, Jeffrey began dreaming of the day when he could sit on the rail cap.

Jeffrey called me up to the bridge. He and Sean had decided that we should anchor that night in a place called Bottleneck Inlet. Its narrow entrance was somewhere up ahead, obscured by the thick trees that line Finlayson Channel.

"You can't see it now, but the opening for Bottleneck is just up ahead," Jeffrey told us as he steered the David B straight toward the shore.

Aaron, Sean and I strained to find the opening, but it was still invisible. Jeffrey checked the chart again to make sure we were on course. As we neared the far side of the channel, we saw a small gap in the forest widen to become the entrance. It didn't seem possible that it would open up enough for there to be an anchorage just beyond.

I went on deck to watch as the gap widened to almost fifty feet. Off to the sides of the boat, the trees clung to the hillside that rose steeply from the water to a height of nearly two thousand feet.

We continued into the inlet. The tide was high, and we easily passed over a one-fathom spot with lots of water to spare under the keel. The cut opened into a slightly wider slot. There were a couple boats already anchored inside, so instead of crowding them, we chose a spot close to the entrance of the bottleneck. Jeffrey stopped the *David B* and carefully spun the boat around in place. It was too narrow to make a circle.

After our noise died away, the Swainson's thrushes began to sing. Their calls echoed from the steep sides of Bottleneck and filled the air. It sounded like there were hundreds of them. I was in heaven. Their song is truly my favorite, and I'd noted to Jeffrey at each anchorage the moment I heard even one. Here there were too many to count. I sat on the trunk cabin with my hands locked around my knees, listening and enjoying the symphony. Jeffrey came out on deck. He smiled and sat down on the rail cap and leaned against the lifelines. He laughed at me for my love of Swainson's thrushes, but I didn't care. Seeing him relaxing on the rail cap after a long day was one of the best rewards for the years of hard work we had put into the boat.

Later that night, after dinner had been served and the galley was clean, I decided it was too nice to go to bed at my usual time. I wanted to stay up. There were so many birds still singing. My watch read 2330, but because we were so far north, the sun had just barely gone down. The air was cool, but it still felt good to be outside. Sean was still up, and we both sat on deck, just listening.

"Do you hear that?" I asked.

"Yeah, it's an owl," Sean whispered. "I think it's over there," he said, pointing to the hillside.

"Yeah, I think you're right," I quietly said back to him.

I can't believe how lucky we are to be here.

CHAPTER 7

WE WERE ON A MISSION FOR FASTENERS

| M/V David B -- Ship's Log | | | | Date | 26 JUNE 2006 |

Time	Location	Wind	Baro	Depth	Remarks
0550	Anchored R. Hbueck	0	1032	51.9	Clear Calm Swainsons Thrushs
1040	Underway from Bottleneck			inlet	
1900	Sainty Pt —Whales —Wind SE 15 kts				
2150	Nettle Basin —Anchored	w	90 ft		

WE LEFT BOTTLENECK on a rising tide. The shallow at the entrance was only six feet at mean low water, and the *David B* draws seven. Leaving when we did gave us the security of knowing that even if our calculations were wrong or the chart was incorrect and we touched bottom, we'd float free as the tide rose. The depth sounder read two feet under the keel as we passed over the shallow entrance. We turned north.

We had another long day ahead that would take us through Princess Royal Channel and into Grenville Channel. The navigation was easy and the water deep. "You hardly even need a chart," Jeffrey proclaimed at one point. "You just need to stay in the center, go straight, and count off the miles as they go by."

We'd been underway for a while when I remembered another charter boat operator telling us to enjoy this trip, because after we were discovered, we'd never have the chance to enjoy the boat as our own again. It was good advice. I tried to soak up as much free time as possible by reading, knitting, and watching the scenery scroll by as we continued toward our destination.

Jeffrey was having a more difficult time relaxing and enjoying the trip. This was partly because the acoustics on the bridge deck changed dramatically depending on where you stood, and leaning to the left or the right would cause you to hear sounds from the engine differently. He was constantly spooked by new phantom engine noises and would often ask, "Does the engine sound different?" If I was in the galley, I'd stop what I was doing, listen to see if there was a new bang, clack, or thud from down below, then look up at him and say "No, there're no new engine sounds down here." Then I'd think to myself, as I'd lock onto a single note of the engine music in the background, *Is that really right? How about that deep banging sound? Was that there before? Yeah, that sound has been there all along. I'm sure I'd notice if something different popped up. I wish I understood the engine more.*

Jeffrey also worried about how much Aaron had to learn about the engine and that with his inexperience, he'd overlook some developing issue. I often would notice Jeffrey holding one of the pilothouse doors halfway open so that it would catch the echo of the exhaust. With his head cocked slightly toward the door, he'd listen to each of the cylinders firing. Then he'd lean back inside and tell Aaron, "It sounds like one of the cylinders is hitting too hard. Can you go down and adjust the offender?" I really didn't understand what they were doing, but Aaron's adjustments kept the engine running smoothly as we continued north.

In the shipyard, I was beginning to understand more about wooden boat building as the *David B* was slowly transformed. The old planks, with their blistered and peeling black paint, were coming off. New beautiful clear-grain ones were waiting to be shaped and fastened on. It was a thrill. The sounds of drills, hammers, and saws combined with the smell of freshly cut wood filled the air. It was obvious: we were breathing new life into the *David B*.

"We need to decide on fasteners," Jeffrey said one evening, soon after the planking stock arrived. As with the foredeck, Jeffrey loved making decisions about fasteners.

"What are our choices, again?" Aaron asked as he was falling asleep on the couch.

"Well I can't decide," Jeffrey said. "We can get some new ones here in town that would need to be galvanized, but if we go to the ship supply place in Anacortes, they have a whole bunch of galvie ones. When I talked with them this afternoon, the guy there says that they have several thousand of them in stock, and their price is pretty good. I think we should use number forty-eight by three and a half, flathead. That'll give us an inch and a half in the plank and two into the frame."

We settled on getting them from the Anacortes Marine Supply and Hardware Co. It's an interesting antique-mall sort of place for old boats and is divided up into three sections. The main room has hardware, fasteners, and finishes for boats and smells faintly of pine tar. In the way that a fast food restaurant pipes out the smell of charbroiled burgers to make you salivate, the smell of an old building and tar makes old sailors itchy with the desire to mess about in boats.

The next two rooms are dedicated to old shit that you really don't need but love looking at. In the middle room, there's a whole section of used nautical dishware, Greek fishermen's hats, army surplus clothing, and random books. This is sort of the catch-all basin for the un-nautical who find themselves here, unsure of what to do while their boat-loving friends finger through the cotton and oakum and read the labels on two-part epoxy clear-coat finishes. The uninitiated might wander into the third room, but a sweeping look at the long tables of bulk oil cups, copper gaskets, and unusual tools causes them to retreat back to the dishes and dusty books they recognize. It's this third room that Jeffrey likes best. Tools, gauges, and an old mini steam engine live in here. You can find anything from a box of cotter pins to firebrick. We usually come here with the hopes that we might find some kind of old-timey treasure. Once in a while, something like a worn-out gauge will catch Jeffrey's eye and he'll smile like a kid on an Easter egg hunt. Jeffrey's a gauge guy. They make him inexplicably happy. But there wasn't time for gauges on this trip, today. We were on a mission for fasteners.

There's also a secret fourth area that only a lucky few will ever see—the basement. It's where they keep things that you have to ask for by name. I don't know what's down there, but I know Jeffrey's been there.

While I looked at the collection of old dishes and mugs adorned with ships' wheels and golden anchors, thinking how nice they'd look in the galley, Jeffrey and Aaron went to talk with the guy in the office, which was styled like an old-time tool crib.

There appeared to be a long discussion of our whole project with the shopkeeper. As I walked up, the shop guy was talking about one of the old Washington state ferries and how it also had a Washington-Estep engine. He was apparently interested in our project and wanted to talk about the finer points of antique engines and how much better they could be than their modern counter parts. The conversation was going well, and it appeared that our project was worthy enough for an invitation to visit the semi-trailer out back where the fasteners were stored. Jeffrey was antsy to get moving but listened politely, knowing that the engine stories were part of our acceptance into a secret society of maritime history that surrounds old workboats. The shopkeeper would get us the right fasteners, but first, in order to be inducted, we needed to discuss old engines.

When the shop guy digressed from the old Washington state ferries and began to talk about the newer ones, Jeffrey made his move.

"Yeah, the old heavy-duties. They sure are nice and will run forever if you take good care of them. They were built so stout. So, do you think we could go have a look at those fasteners?"

"The fasteners, right, follow me. This way." The shopkeeper motioned to us, and we went single file down a narrow passage and through a door into a low, junk-filled space. Then we ducked through another door to the bright sunshine of the outside. Sitting in a weedy lot behind the building were four or five old trailer rigs that had clearly been there for some time. The shopkeeper walked up to one and unlocked it. He rooted around inside and soon emerged with a wooden crate of treasure—the perfect screws for the job. He opened the crate with a crowbar and handed Jeffrey a smallish box. I felt out of step with time, standing around in my polar fleece jacket. The trailer, the crate, and the shopkeeper were preserved from some bygone era. The scene that was playing out before me seemed more like a black-and-white movie about the history of wooden boat building than a part of my life. I looked over to Jeffrey, who seemed to blend easily between the historic and modern. He was fondling the cardboard box that had held the fasteners for the last five decades.

"How many crates do you have back there?" Jeffrey asked.

"More than enough. How many do you want?"

"I think four crates will do," Jeffrey said, then asked Aaron and me, as more of an afterthought, "Is this all right?"

We agreed that these were the fasteners for us, and I left to get the car while Jeffrey and Aaron settled up.

When I returned, Jeffrey was admiring the crates. "Check these out," he said, setting one of them into the trunk of our Geo Prizm. "You just don't see packaging like this anymore. These crates are amazing. Look at the tight grain of the wood. You would never use old growth for a packing crate any more. Things were so different back then."

We'd been underway in Princess Royal Channel for a couple hours when we came up to a cookie-bite of a cove containing the remains of the ghost cannery of Butedale. Jeffrey asked Aaron to slow us down so we could have a closer look. We drifted in the cove, taking in all that remained of Butedale. At first glance, it seemed as if a tornado or earthquake had singled out this outpost with sudden wrath, but actually the once-vibrant cannery was quietly succumbing to the slow decay of abandonment. Several buildings had holes in their roofs, and others were collapsed on their foundations. Seedlings of spruce and hemlock sprouted from the moss-covered rooftops. I admired the tenacity of the forest and its ability to erase the memory of human settlements. There was, however, a sign that Butedale was not fully abandoned; a curl of smoke was coming from the chimney of one of the better-maintained buildings.

"I wish we had time to stop. The Chart Reverend back in Nanaimo said that the guy living here's a squatter, but the guys on the tugboats said he was a caretaker." Jeffrey nosed the *David B* further into the cove and toward a voluminous waterfall.

"Really? The place looks sketchy," I said.

"Yeah, but think of all the cool crap that's there. Check out the waterfall. One of the tugboat captains I worked with said it used to power the whole place when it was a cannery. It was abandoned years ago, but the hydropower generator kept making electricity and they left all the lights on. They say that it was creepy to drive past the decaying buildings of Butedale all brightly lit in the middle of nowhere."

"It seems like a good place for a resort. I see on the chart that there's a big lake back behind that ridge up there, and I've seen a couple of sport-fishing boats today, so I bet the fishing's good," I said.

"Yeah, I guess it's been tried before, but maybe it's just too big of a project to make it work," he said as we backed away from the waterfall. His words made me wonder whether the *David B* was also too big of a project to work. Sure, we were cruising to Alaska, but the rebuild had depleted all of our financial resources. It felt as if we were in a race between being discovered and going bankrupt. Every day, I waited for the phone to ring, hoping that we'd get another reservation.

I thought for a while about our rebuild while Butedale passed into the distance. *It wasn't that long ago that the* David B *would have fit in nicely with Butedale's ambience of rot, decay, and reclamation by nature.* The bunkhouse with the tree growing out of its roof showed how quickly nature reclaims what we don't take care of.

By our third month in the shipyard, we had become a regular fixture. Greg had finished the rim log, and Jeffrey and Aaron had installed all of the new frames. We had a new saying about the boat: "Every day, a little better." Jeffrey and I would tell each other that in the morning when we woke up and in the evening before we went to bed. The mantra seemed to be working. We had finished removing the old hull planking from the back of the boat. The new frames were radiant next to the old ones. We didn't have any reason to remove the original frames, so they remained on the boat: relics.

The first new hull plank was a monumental day for us. It symbolized the peak of the rebuild. With this one piece of wood and a few fasteners, we were starting to close the boat back up. We were done taking the boat apart and done with rotten wood. From here on, we were putting the *David B* back together. It was an important enough day that Aaron's dad, Jack, came over from Leavenworth so he could see the first plank go on. I wanted to be there too.

To steam the plank, we rented an industrial diesel-powered steam cleaner/pressure washer that we hooked up to a long steam box that we had borrowed from the shipyard. There was a lot of standing around while we waited for the plank to cook. It takes about an hour for every inch of thickness, and our plank was two and a quarter inches thick, so it was ready after two hours and fifteen minutes.

"So, here's what we are going to do," Jeffrey told us. "When the plank comes out, Aaron and I will carry it over to the boat. Jack, I'll need your help holding it up while Aaron clamps it against the frames. I have all the clamps hanging there. Once the plank is cool, I'll drill the holes for the fasteners, and then Aaron'll come behind me with the impact driver and set the screws."

"How much time do you have to get it in place after you pull the plank from the steam box?" Jack asked.

"Not much. We've got to get it on the boat in a hurry. We only have a few minutes."

Jack looked around, nodding his head. It was a bit of an obstacle course to get the plank from the box, through the door of the cover, under the ladder, and between all the jack-stands that held the *David B* upright.

"So I think we're ready," Jeffrey said, checking his watch.

I gave him a nervous smile. The first plank was nine feet long and was going in low on the hull. None of us had ever done this before.

Jeffrey and Aaron put on leather welder's gloves and opened the box. Steam obscured my view of them. The plank was still stiff, not noodley as the process implies. I followed them around the obstacle course from the steam box to the back of the boat.

"Jack, come over here and help hold the plank up against the hull right where I am," Jeffrey said. "Aaron, you got that clamp?"

The hot steaming wood easily conformed to the shape of the hull with the pressure of the clamps.

When Jeffrey was happy with how the plank was aligned, he went to work making the holes for the screws. As he finished, Aaron came along with the impact driver and set the screws. The excitement and the sounds of the drill and then the impact driver made it seem like an Indy pit stop. Instead of the smell of hot tires, however, we worked with the sweet smell of steamy wood.

It was all over in a matter of minutes: Our first plank was in place. There were high-fives all around. With this plank in place, we felt that we would be out of the shipyard in no time. The demolition process was finished, and from here on out, we would be going forward.

With Butedale far behind, we entered the crossroads of Wright Sound, where Princess Royal Channel ends and Grenville Channel begins. We were about two hours away from our stop for the night when we noticed a single fishing boat several miles behind us. By the time we made our turn into Lowe Inlet, our anchorage for the night, it had caught up to us. The skipper apparently knew exactly where he wanted to anchor and passed us in an all-fired hurry as we rounded Pike Point and entered Nettle Basin.

"He's going to take the spot I wanted, isn't he?" Jeffrey complained.

"Looks like it," Sean replied.

"All right, then, I guess we can anchor a bit deeper than he can. I hate getting corked on a parking spot." Jeffrey turned to look over at the chart plotter to see what his second choice for anchoring was. "There's a five-two spot just around the peninsula. I guess we can take that instead."

Aaron dropped the anchor and then shut down the engine. Besides the fishing boat, there were three or four other boats anchored. The sides of Nettle Basin are about two thousand feet high, and the air was very still.

After dinner, I sat up in the pilothouse watching a moose that had wandered down to the shore. I was in the seat next to the chart plotter and noted the GPS track on the computer screen. It showed that we had been slowly swinging in a small half circle. When the tide changed, we'd make the other half. It looked nice and tight, meaning that the anchor was doing its job and that we would sleep worry-free.

In the middle of the night, the wind started blowing. I lay awake listening. The gusts seemed to be coming from the high hillside across the basin. As the wind roared downhill, it hit the water and splayed across our anchorage before impacting the boat. *Williwaws*, I thought in the dark as I felt the boat shudder. After the wind rushed past us, it sounded like it pushed up the other hillside and ran out of steam. There would be a moment of calm, then we'd be hit again with another strong gust. Even though I knew that we had a four-hundred-fifty-pound anchor on the bottom with a good five hundred pounds of chain on top of that, I still worried that we were dragging anchor.

"Are you awake?" Jeffrey asked as I moved to get up.

"Yeah," I said. "I'm going to go check on things. The wind makes me uneasy. I'm sure it's all right, but I just can't sleep."

I climbed the ladder. The pilothouse was still warm from the stove, and the red nightlights made me feel more cozy and secure. I checked the chart plotter. It showed the same tight half-circle of breadcrumbs on the screen. We hadn't moved out of position, so things were good. I leaned on the wheel and looked out the window. I watched the anchor lights of the other boats dance as each new williwaw arrived.

I noticed that the fishing boat that had corked us on the prime anchoring spot was closer than I remembered. With each gust coming from the far side of the basin, the fishing boat drew nearer. After a while, I went down to get Jeffrey.

"What's up? Is everything okay?" he asked when I walked into our cabin.

"Yeah, *we're* fine, but I think the fish boat's dragging anchor. Can you come up and have a look? I'm not sure what to do," I said. I could hear in his sleepy voice that he was reluctant to get out of our warm, comfortable bed.

"Sure, I'll come up."

The williwaws continued to come in pulses, roaring through the trees. We could see small white caps in the black of the water as we watched the fishing boat meander around the anchorage.

"Wow, he's getting pretty close. Have you been able to see if anyone's awake onboard?" Jeffrey asked.

"No, I think he's sleeping like a baby," I said.

"Let's get a couple of fenders out and set them in the skiff. If he gets closer, we can fend him off then. I'm a little worried that his anchor might be getting tangled in with ours," he said as we went out on deck.

"I think it's gusting at least to fifty," Jeffrey half shouted as we gathered the fenders. It was hard to hear him, and we hurried back inside.

With each strong gust, the fishing boat inched closer. I looked at the clock and it was almost 0300. The boat seemed ghostly as it wandered around in the middle of the night. Jeffrey decided to spend the rest of the night sleeping on the settee while I kept watch. I added more wood to the embers in the stove to start it back up. The warmth chased away my fear that something would go wrong. I snuggled up in the corner of the settee opposite Jeffrey to watch and wait.

A strong gust came rolling down the hillside. I could see the waves rippling across the water as it came toward us. It was time to wake up Jeffrey and fend off the fishing boat. We stood outside with our fenders hanging down. My long hair flew wildly in the wind, hitting me in my eyes. The boat was almost close enough to touch. The wind pushed a little harder. It came closer. A gust came from a different direction and pushed him away. We watched his boat swing toward the others and waited for its return. The next williwaw wasn't as strong, and the fishing boat didn't come as close. We relaxed a little and rushed inside. We watched as the williwaws rolled through, each a little less than the one before. We had escaped a midnight collision with the fish boat. Jeffrey lay back down on the settee to get a little sleep. It was beginning to get light.

CHAPTER 8

SHREDD'N THE GNAR-GNAR

Time	Location	Wind	Baro	Depth	Remarks
0555	Anchored Lowe Holbush Inlet	zero	10.8	87ft	Windy - Just Got Nearby Draggin Ahead
0605	Weighed Anchor				Clear
1600	Secure Prince Rupert	West Face of Dock			

M/V David B - Ship's Log Date 6/27/06

WE GOT TO PRINCE RUPERT late that afternoon, after being underway for almost eight hours. Jeffrey and I were still tired from our long night of worrying in Lowe Inlet, and were happy to be tied up at the Prince Rupert Rowing and Yacht Club.

At the top of the dock was a pub called the Breakers that served cheeseburgers and beer and offered a slow but free wireless connection. We wandered in for just one beer and decided to stay for dinner and celebrate our last night in Canada. We had a view of the marina and the *David B* out the pub's large windows. The sun was warm through the glass, and I watched the boat's green pennant wave gently in the wind. I still felt disbelief that we were here—a day away from Alaska.

"Ya know," I interrupted the guys' conversation, "it was only a little over a year ago that the *David B* was in the shipyard."

Our table was quiet for a moment, each one of us looking out at the boat.

In that moment of silence, hundreds of scenes of our time in the yard flashed through my mind.

"Was it really just a year ago that we launched?" Jeffrey asked.

"Yeah, just a little over a year. Remember, you did the road-bike leg of Ski to Sea the next morning," I said.

"Yeah, I know, but it doesn't seem possible that we could have gotten everything done in that short of a time."

I thought about the last year. *Hard to believe that just six months ago we hadn't even started on the interior. I could stand at the bulkhead to the anchor chain locker at the front of the boat and see all the way past the engine to the back of the boat.*

"Remember how worried you were about the final survey?" Jeffrey chided me.

"Don't tease me. I *was* really worried that the insurance company would find something wrong with the boat, and that we would have done all the work and still not be able to get insurance."

"What did you think would happen?" Sean asked.

"I don't know," I said. "I just don't trust them, and I worried that they would prevent us from starting this business if we couldn't insure the boat. I was shaking so bad when the survey came in the mail. I was convinced that there would be something in there that would condemn us."

"Were you that worried, too?" Sean asked Jeffrey.

"Not like Christine was. I'd been working with the surveyor and we'd done most everything on his list, so I felt confident that the survey would go well."

"When we got it, we quickly scanned through it looking for any indication that we wouldn't be able to get insurance," I said.

"What did the surveyor say, exactly?" Sean asked.

"The usual stuff," Jeffrey said. "He had some recommendations of things we'd need to do in the future, but overall he said we'd done a good job and the boat was in good condition."

"The best part was that he complimented Jeffrey on his skill as a shipwright on the last page. I was so excited for Jeffrey to call the insurance company. I think it was the first time in my life I'd ever felt that way. I hate insurance."

"So was it easy to get insurance after the survey?"

Jeffrey and I both laughed, and Jeffrey continued the story. "Well, Captain Tim had given me the name of the guy he said the *Schooner Martha* uses. So I called up the guy, told him that I had a sixty-five-foot wooden charter boat that I wanted to insure, and he flat-out lied to me and said he didn't insure wood boats."

"He did what?" Sean exclaimed.

"Yeah, he said that his company did not insure wooden boats, right after I had introduced myself and said I'd gotten his name from Tim."

"So then what?"

"Well, Christine was freaking out that we'd never find an insurance company, and Aaron stayed out of it—"

"Damn straight, I did," Aaron interrupted.

"So I kept looking. I knew someone out there would eventually want to take our money."

"When he did find someone," I said, "I practically jumped out of my skin I, was so happy. I couldn't wait to get a check to them and get out of the shipyard."

As the waitress brought our hamburgers, I looked back out at the *David B* in the marina and thought about the past year. The pennant was still waving in the light breeze.

Launching the boat from the shipyard that first time was a huge thrill, but, like so much that happened that year, it seemed like it was all happening too fast. We'd filed a copy of our brand-new insurance policy at the Port of Bellingham, so we were free to go back to our slip whenever we wanted, but I didn't feel we were ready. I knew Jeffrey was anxious to get the boat back because the cost of staying in the shipyard was so high, but it still surprised me when he made an appointment to launch the boat right away. To anyone else, the *David B* looked far from ready to go back into the water.

"We're gonna splash next Saturday," Jeffrey said, smiling.

"Seriously? Don't you think that's rushing things? There's still so much to do. What about the bulwarks and sanding and painting the hull? Don't forget you're signed up to race the next morning. Are you all right with it being the day before Ski to Sea? You need to leave around five-thirty or six the next morning, that Sunday, to be at the run-bike exchange. Wouldn't Monday be a better day?"

"No, Monday's Memorial Day and the yard won't be open. I think Saturday will work fine. As far as the work that needs to be done, we're finished with everything below the water line other than paint. We can do everything else when we're back at the dock."

Our workdays that last week at the shipyard got longer and longer. By midweek, we were working from five in the morning until nine at night. I gardened for seven or eight hours each day, then drove to the yard to sand and paint. There was no time to cook, so we ate pizza. When we didn't order it ourselves, friends and neighbors would stop by with it. Then they'd spend a few hours painting with us. I never thought I could ever tire of pizza, but I did that week. The feeling of nearing our launching date was electric. The best day was when we removed the cover. Seeing the whole boat for the first time in almost six months gave me shivers. Its hull was beautiful, especially the stern, where most of the new construction had taken place.

✷

The day before we were to launch the boat, Jeffrey was called into the office at the shipyard. They were sure we weren't ready and wanted us to reschedule, but Jeffrey insisted that we were. It seemed funny to me that they didn't want us in the yard when we hauled, and now they didn't want us to leave.

We continued our mad rush to get the last details of our shipyard time finished. We worked on painting, frames, planking, and thru-hulls. Aaron spent hours polishing the propeller. Jeffrey went over his lists again and again to make sure we had everything finished and there wouldn't be some important detail left behind.

On Friday, as the daylight faded, we worked into the dark by shop lights to finish the last coat of topside paint. Just after eleven p.m., Jeffrey called for us to stop work. Like students cramming for a final exam, we had finally had enough. The *David B* sat silently in the dark, shining with new paint, new frames, new planking, and a second life.

I snapped a picture that would forever sum up our last day in the shipyard. It's really nothing special, just a bunch of guys standing around in the dark with beer bottles in their hands. The boat isn't even in the photo. I love the image for what it means to me, the moment in time where the balance shifted. In that instant on May 27, 2005, we all stood back and took in the work we had done. We had saved the *David B*.

I felt apprehensive about the *David B* going into the water. We expected the boat to leak for a while until the planks swelled from constant immersion, but we were not sure how much. Just in case, Jeffrey had readied and stowed the emergency pump that I had used so many years earlier to save the boat from sinking at the dock.

When I arrived Saturday morning at the yard, the TraveLift was just backing into place. The *David B's* black hull sparkled with its new paint. The propeller that Aaron had spent so much time polishing glowed. The driver maneuvered the lift with a remote-control pack that he wore on his chest. He walked around the boat, pressing levers on his remote until the lift was correctly positioned, then shut it down so that the shipyard workers could get the slings hooked up. It was a hot day, and we stood in the shade of the building next to the *David B*.

My pulse quickened as the TraveLift roared back to life. The driver took up on the slings just enough to make them snug against the boat's hull. He inspected each one carefully. I naively worried that the slings wouldn't hold and the boat would fall. I crossed my fingers for good luck. When everything checked out, he began to lift. Above the roar of the engine, I could hear the *David B* creak and moan as the slings constricted around her. She lifted clear of her blocking and was finally free of the land. We walked alongside, parade-like, as she rolled slowly toward the sea.

People all over the yard stopped what they were doing when they saw that the *David B* was about to be launched. Our procession to the water was a proud moment, and although she wasn't completely finished, the *David B* looked beautiful. A few people even clapped for us.

The TraveLift rolled out on the long piers and lowered the *David B* so that her deck was even with the parking lot. It dangled only a few feet above the water as we stepped aboard.

"What do you think, Captain?" the driver shouted, moving his hearing protectors to the side and then cupping his hand around his free ear.

"I think we're all good!" Jeffrey shouted back. He gave the driver a big smile and a thumbs-up. "What do you think, guys? Are we?" He didn't wait for our response. "There's no use just hanging here," he said, more to himself than to his crew. "Lower away!" he shouted back up to the TraveLift driver.

As the boat was lowered into the water, Jeffrey disappeared belowdecks with his flashlight. I stood near the scuttle and strained to listen for any alarm that Jeffrey might yell out. The noisy TraveLift engine and the creaking of the *David B's* timbers made it hard to hear. We stopped moving, and the driver took the lift's engine out of gear. We were in the water and done with the shipyard.

The morning air in Prince Rupert was still fresh at 0638 when we cast our lines from the Prince Rupert Rowing and Yacht Club.

"Do you think you'll run Venn Passage?" Sean asked, after he'd stowed the dock lines.

"I don't see why not. If we take Venn, then it's only a twelve-hour day, whereas if we backtrack and go down around Digby Island, we'll end up with a fifteen-hour day. I'm hoping to be secure in Ketchikan in time for dinner tonight," Jeffrey said, his voice almost cracking with excitement.

The entrance to Venn Passage was about two miles away, and as we motored across the harbor, we were surprised by how busy it was. There appeared to be a salmon opening—what commercial fishermen call a day within the fishing season when the government says that they can fish—and it seemed that everything that floated in Prince Rupert was heading for the same spot.

"Sean, can you watch the GPS and make sure we're on track? Christine and Aaron, can each of you keep watching for markers?" Jeffrey said, a little nervously, as we crowded in toward the first set of buoys.

"The first one will be on your port side off Grindstone Point," Sean reported, "and the next one is a green. It will be off your starboard."

Aaron and I began scanning for the markers. Jeffrey looked over his shoulder at the chart plotter to confirm our position. We were in the center of the shallow channel that's between the mainland and Digby Island. Two or three smaller fishing boats were quickly gaining on us. It looked as if they'd catch us at the first turn.

"What's the saying to remember which side of the buoys we need to be on?" Aaron asked.

"'Red, right returning,' but we're heading out to sea instead of returning, so the reds will be on our left," Sean explained. "Then there's also 'even red nuns carry odd green cans,' for the numbering of the markers."

"Got it. I see the 'QR' red marker, up on the left ahead of that dock up there," Aaron said, looking through the binoculars and pointing at it so Jeffrey could get a visual.

"Hey, Jeffrey, it looks like you've got a water taxi coming up behind you as well. It's a ways back yet, but I think it will catch us somewhere near that corner up ahead," I said.

"Thanks, roger that," Jeffrey acknowledged.

The channel was about six hundred feet across at the 'QR' marker. The first dogleg, where it looked like the water taxi would catch us, was three hundred feet across, but with so many fishing boats and the water taxi converging at the same time, it felt closer to thirty feet. The excitement built in the pilothouse as Aaron, Sean, and I called out marker locations and watched for boats.

"After the 'QR' we'll need to line up on a range board. There's also a green can about a quarter of a mile past the 'QR' marker. Once you pass that, you'll want to line up on the range board," Sean said.

"Roger, Roger," Jeffrey said, clearly enjoying the slalom-like quality of Venn Passage with its markers, nuns, cans, range boards, ferries, and fish boats.

"The water taxi's setting up to pass you on the starboard," I said.

"Where are those fish boats?" Jeffrey asked.

"There's one in your blind spot on your starboard and two a little further back," Aaron said.

"Keep an eye on them." Jeffrey quickly looked back to the galley. "Christine, is everything secure back there? If the water taxi is the same one I saw in Prince Rupert, then we're in for a good-sized wake."

"Yeah, I think everything is all good, but I'll go down and double check."

I stepped off the bridge deck and checked for anything left lying around on the galley table. Outside, the water taxi was catching up to us. It was long and low, and its engine seemed to growl as it approached. The curl of water on its bow was high as it sped toward us, leaving a surprisingly large wake in its path. I looked around the galley one more time. The taxi was going to have to pass close to us, right at the narrow bend in the channel ahead. At the same time, Jeffrey needed to get a sighting of the range boards on shore so he could complete the turn and stay in deep water.

"This is like shredd'n the gnar-gnar," Sean said.

"The gnar-what?" Aaron laughed.

"You know, the gnar-gnar. Like when you're cruising along on your skis and you hit some gnarly shit. I first heard it from the kids when I was captain on the *Schooner Lavengro*. The gnar-gnar, huh?"

"Uh-huh," Aaron said slowly and with a smile.

Sean returned his focus to the chart plotter.

Just as the taxi sped past us, the fish boats caught up to the *David B*. We all rolled around in the taxi's wake. I could hear the sounds of fishing gear clanking on the boat on our starboard side. I waved to the driver, who was near enough that I could have shaken his hand.

"What's next?" Jeffrey asked

"Marker D85," Sean replied.

"Roger that. Are there more fish boats coming up?" Jeffrey asked.

"Yeah, looks like there are several more coming," Sean said with his head sticking out of the pilothouse door.

The next section was just under a mile long and widened out just slightly. The first wave of fish boats had passed us. The water in the channel was choppy with wakes. There was another set of range boards to line up on, and more boats were coming up behind us.

"You'll want to be to the right as much as possible at the next corner," Sean said. "There's a one-meter-eight spot at the turn. Once you're past that marker, you're almost home free. Just watch for the rock at marker 'DJ.'"

We made the turn, along with several other boats. About this time, a group of smaller and faster sport-fishing boats came flying through Venn Passage, their salmon nets flying stretched out like pennants, ready to catch butterflies. The channel narrowed again just past the native village of Metlakatla, the destination of the water taxi we'd seen earlier. We continued on through the channel, working together as a crew. As we neared the end, the passage opened up into Chatham Sound. It was congested with fishing boats setting their nets, and hundreds of rhinoceros auklets, common murres, and pigeon guillemots floated on the surface of the salmon-rich waters. We picked our way through the maze of nets and safely turned north. There were high-fives all around.

"Way to shred the gnar-gnar, guys," Jeffrey laughed.

After congratulating ourselves on navigating our way through Venn Passage, we settled down for a few hours. I happily watched seabirds while keeping an eye out for occasional salmon nets set across our path. Jeffrey had asked Sean to double check that every thing on deck was secure, since we'd be spending a few hours exposed to the swells from Dixon Entrance.

As we neared the border, our anticipation of crossing into Alaska built. Sean counted down our remaining minutes in Canada. I went to the engine room to make sure that Aaron wouldn't miss it. When I returned, Sean zoomed in on the plotter screen to get a better view of the blue cartoon-like triangle that represented the *David B* on the chart. We wanted to watch the green dot in the middle of the triangle touch the line that marked the border between Canada and the United States.

"Okay, guys. Ten"—Sean began, and the rest of us joined in—"nine, eight, seven, six, five, four, three, two . . . One!" We all shouted in unison. Jeffrey reached up and sounded the horn. It boomed across the water and we cheered again.

Jeffrey put his arms around me. I looked up at him. "We're in Alaska!"

THINGS WILL CHANGE

M/V David B -- Ship's Log   Date _28 June 06_

Time	Location	Wind	Baro	Depth	Remarks
0638	UNDERWAY PRINCE RUPERT				• MAKE HARDWARE STORE LIST
1830	SECURE KETCHIKAN	ALASKA			• GET GROCERIES • CHECK FUEL LEVELS

KETCHIKAN IS A LONG, narrow town that's built on a slender strip of low land and extends into Tongass Narrows on piers. Snowcapped mountains rise steeply behind the town. We slowly cruised along the waterfront, past the cruise ship terminals and beyond the fish processing plants to the Bar Harbor Boat Basin, where we the harbormaster had assigned us a slip. The gradual change of the town's waterfront from tourist center to working waterfront was interesting. While Ketchikan relies heavily on tourism, it still stays true to its historic fishing roots. We found our slip, docked, and waited for the Customs agent to clear us into the U.S. While we sat on deck waiting, we planned to walk the mile or so back to the tourist district.

Once cleared, we headed up the dock and turned right onto the sidewalk. It felt good to be walking. Past a new-looking plaza with a supermarket, the sidewalk narrowed, and I noticed that on the waterside there were many places with a four- to six-inch gap between the sidewalk and old piers. The land along the waterfront is so narrow that sections of the street are built out over the water. To cover up the gap, wooden planks were placed in front of doorways. As we walked, employees from the fish processing plants, dressed in long white overcoats and hairnets, would occasionally zip across the sidewalk in forklifts to load seafood into the noisy refrigerated semi-trailers that lined the street. Their grey rubber boots distinguished them from fishermen, who always wear the brown Xtratuf boots.

While we walked, there was a constant buzz of floatplanes taking off and landing. Each plane was laden with passengers from the three cruise ships that lined Ketchikan's waterfront like a fortress wall. I had become accustomed to the quiet of the wilderness, and the sound of the float planes made me think of giant mosquitoes. About halfway through the walk, I began to feel slightly nauseous from the combination of cars, tour buses, construction noise, slow-moving oversized tourists and the endless noise from floatplanes and refrigerated trucks. It didn't help that I was also feeling a gentle "land-rock" from being on a boat for two weeks. There was way too much stimulation, and I felt drunk taking it all in. I had gotten used to a simple, quiet life aboard the *David B* and had temporarily forgotten how busy and noisy humans can be. I couldn't wait to get out of Ketchikan and back into the quiet routine of the boat.

We wandered around looking at the souvenir stores for a while, then stopped for some dinner. The food was good enough but priced for tourists. The restaurant was loud and filled with commotion and distracting televisions, so our conversion during dinner was short and sporadic. The main topic was the arrival of our naturalist.

"So where did you find this guy, again?" Sean asked. We'd only vaguely talked about picking Steven up in Ketchikan. There had been so much to do that we had never really ironed out the details surrounding Steven.

"Jeffrey found him online," I answered, trying my best to drag my eyes away from the moving pictures of the television screen to give Sean proper respect.

"I was looking for a picture of a calving glacier for the website and sent him an e-mail to ask what it would cost to use his on our website, and he said a thousand dollars. I told him we weren't interested and thought that was the end of it. Then a few days later he sent another e-mail saying that he'd gone to our website and could see that we were a small start-up. He wanted to go on a trip in exchange for the use of the image and offered to be our naturalist."

I listened to Jeffrey and Sean talk about how Steven was a wildlife photographer who'd had lots of experience in the Alaskan wilderness and how that would benefit our passengers' experience.

When Steven had first tossed out the idea of joining us, I was skeptical. We didn't know anything about who he was or what he was like, but in conversations with Jeffrey over the phone, he seemed like he'd be a good guy to have on board.

"What time does he arrive?" Sean asked.

"I need to walk over to the airport to meet him at one o'clock tomorrow. We'll leave after he's on board. I think it's only about four hours or so to Meyers Chuck," Jeffrey said.

We paid our bill and then stopped in at a couple of bars to make sure we had really *seen* Ketchikan before walking back to the boat.

There's an expression used by women seeking men in Alaska, where men used to outnumber women by a ratio of five to one: "The odds are good, but the goods are odd." That pretty much summed up our newest crew member. On the surface he seemed normal, but a few sentences into my first conversation with him, I thought we might have made a mistake. I couldn't quite pinpoint what was "off" about Steven, but I just knew there was something.

I was cleaning the fridge on the back deck when Jeffrey first brought him around to meet me and Sean, who was helping me organize the dairy products. Steven was tall and husky, with straight hair that was thin on top. He looked a little monkish. I tried to make small talk, but the constant revving of floatplane engines made it difficult. He looked around the boat a bit, then went below to stow his belongings.

"So what's he like?" I asked Jeffrey in a hushed tone during a lull in the air traffic.

"Well, I think he's all right. His laugh is a little annoying and he seemed a bit nervous. I have a feeling he doesn't spend much time around other people. It sounds like he works in the field, mostly taking pictures of bears and heavy equipment," Jeffrey said.

"I don't like him," Sean said immediately.

"Really? Why?" Jeffrey asked.

"I don't know. There's just something kind of off about him," he said.

"Christine, what do you think?" Jeffrey turned toward me to gauge my first impressions.

"I don't know. I didn't much like his laugh, and he did seem a bit nervous. Maybe when he's had some time to settle in and we get to know him better, I'll have a better impression of him," I said.

"Hmm," Jeffrey breathed out. "So, how much longer are you two going to be at this? Will you be ready to get underway in a half hour or so?

"Yeah, we can go when ever you like. Sean's got most everything that needs to go in the fridge put away and I just need to finish reorganizing the freezer," I said.

We left Ketchikan a little after 1530, and after all the lines were stowed, I decided it was time to finally try out Whiskey Golf. I added two cups of the starter to a bowl and scraped a little of it from the spoon to taste. It was sharp and young. I imagined what it would taste like in the finished loaf. *It will be good,* I thought, *although it might not taste as rich or full of flavor as an older sourdough. In time, Whiskey Golf's gonna make the best breads.* I continued making the dough by mixing in the water, sugar, olive oil, flour, and salt before turning the dough out onto the counter, where I kneaded the bread dough rhythmically to the beat of the engine. I gathered up the dough, folded it, and pressed my palms deep into it. With each knead, I felt it change and become more smooth and elastic.

While I worked in the galley, I listened to the conversation that Steven was having with the guys on the bridge deck. In his words I searched for clues as to how he would fit in with us as crew. My first clue came later that night while we were at anchor in Meyers Chuck. We'd finished dinner and were in the middle of discussing how good my first loaf of bread from the Whiskey Golf starter was when I got up to gather plates and wash the dishes. Steven volunteered to help, and since I never turn down help with after-dinner galley cleanup, I was happy to accept his offer.

"You can scrape them off into the trash and then stack them on the counter," I said, organizing plates, glasses and cutlery.

"Hey, hey, wait. You want to throw away all the food on people's plates?" Steven said.

"Uh, well, yeah." I was confused by the question. I didn't know whether he was joking or not.

"That's good food. I'll eat it." He took back his fork and piled leftover salad and risotto from each of our plates onto his. "I'm not really all that hungry now, but don't throw this away. It's too good to be wasted, and you can't just waste food."

I cocked my head to the side a bit to let his words and actions sink in. There wasn't all that much left, and I really didn't want to save it since the fridge was packed full. I played along to be nice, got out the cling wrap, and covered his plate to put into the fridge, knowing full well that he'd never get around to eating it.

When I returned from the fridge on the back deck, Steven was standing in the middle of the galley awaiting instructions. I walked up to the galley table and asked Sean, Jeffrey, and Aaron to gather the rest of the dishes.

"Wait, wait, wait," Steven said, stepping in front of me before anyone could touch a plate. "Don't stack those plates. If you do, you'll have to wash the backs of them."

"You've got to be kidding," Sean laughed, but Steven was serious. He didn't want to waste water or time on washing the backs of dinner plates.

"I know at home it's okay to wash just the faces of your plates, but we need to be a little more sanitary here." I wondered if there was a way to relieve Steven from dish duty. "Sean, can you stack and pass Steven the plates?" I exercised my right as Chef to demand that dishes be washed my way.

While I organized the pots and pans and took the stacked dishes to a reluctant Steven, I explained my methodology for dishwashing on the boat. It might seem trivial to some, but washing dishes in a small galley needs to be choreographed. I explained that the space is limited, and to be efficient, I put the dishes in piles so I can wash all the like items together, dry them, and put them away. I tried to calm Steven's fear of wasting water by explaining that even though I wanted to make sure we used plenty of water to wash the dishes, I didn't want to just let it run down the sink. I showed him how to organize the cutlery into a pan to let it soak. I separated dishes from pots and pans and placed glasses in the dishpan with a generous amount of Joy. As the hot water and Joy bubbled in the dishpan, I looked around for orphan dishes that had not made it into the galley. Steven stood by, nervously waiting for me to turn off the water. I took my time and even let the dish tub fill a little more than normal. I wanted to make sure that if Steven *was* going to wash dishes, it would be on my terms.

"Aren't you worried about how much water we have on board?" he asked, seeing the mound of bubbles clear the top of the sink.

"We have several hundred gallons, and we'll be making a stop in Petersburg the day after tomorrow. We'll refill the tanks there and that should get us all the way to Juneau," I said. "I don't think we're wasting water. Besides, above all things in the galley, the dishes must be clean and sanitary, and if that takes a little bit more water, then so be it." I had no intention of having greasy smeared plates that had not been fully cleaned just for the sake of saving a little water.

"How about if I wash and you dry, since I don't know where everything goes?" Steven offered.

I went to the settee and pulled back a seat cushion to get a dishrag. I looked over at Aaron, who was still trying to keep a straight face about my handling of the situation.

As Steven washed the glasses, I inspected each one to make sure it was clean. I had a feeling he had "bachelor rules" for housekeeping, and I didn't completely trust him. I certainly appreciated the help and the effort, but I wished I could just work on my own.

I looked back at the settee again and caught Sean snickering behind his laptop as he downloaded his pictures from his camera.

Once the dishes were washed and the galley clean, I went down below to read. I opened my book and listened to the muffled voices from above filter down to me.

Instead of reading, I found myself thinking about Sean's contributions to the *David B* and his uneasiness with Steven. I'd grown to trust and rely on Sean to be there, and he'd helped us a lot to get through the last few months.

In mid-January 2006, we got our first reservation. It came in the form of an e-mail from Australia. A group of four signed up for a trip between Juneau and Ketchikan. Jeffrey and I were over the moon with excitement. It seemed like passengers would be easy to find and the boat would start paying its own bills. I dreamed of us selling out all of our bunks and not having the constant day-to-day worry of whether or not we were going to bounce our checking account or have to borrow more money from a credit card to pay our bills.

The main problem we had when we got our first reservation was that the boat was far from finished. The exterior projects were mostly done, but the interior of the boat was still a void. With the exception of the engine, there was nothing between the anchor chain locker and the rudder post.

"So I think we should give ourselves a deadline. What do you think?" Jeffrey said one morning while the two of us went over our daily to-do list.

"I think that's a really good idea. Do you think you, me, and Aaron can get all the cabins, plumbing, electrical, and painting done on our own in time to leave for Alaska? We have to leave Bellingham by June eighteenth to be in Juneau on time with a couple of days to spare in case something goes sideways."

"I'd like to be done sooner than that, and I've been thinking that there's too much to do and we're going to need help. So, how do you feel about us hiring Sean to work on the cabins? Also, Aaron said the other day that his friend Dan's an electrician and would probably help do the wiring. We could hire him, too."

I sighed and looked down at the papers in front of Jeffrey. The top page was single-spaced and had two columns. There were several headings, each titled for a certain part of the project. It was just the first page of the to-do list. I lifted the top sheet for no real reason, just to confirm that the list went on. I sat back in my chair, mulling over what it would cost to add labor to the project. We were already in the hole, so going into debt wasn't the problem. How far was now the question.

"When do you want the boat to be ready?" I asked.

"April, in case we get any reservations for the San Juan Islands trips in May," he said, and waited for my answer.

"You know that's only three months away?"

"Yeah, that's why I want to hire Sean."

"I know. I can see how much needs to be done and that without help we won't make it. When do you think he can start?"

"I don't know. I'll give him a call today."

✦

Sean agreed to start working on the carpentry for the *David B*'s cabins in two weeks. He would have started sooner, but Jeffrey and Aaron needed to install the new fuel tanks and we weren't done with the final layout of the cabins.

Jeffrey and I had spent years talking about where there would be cabins, but we'd never really gotten around to putting it down on paper. Now that it was time to actually build the cabins, Jeffrey decided to involve Aaron as well.

"So, we're going to play a little game tonight."

"Oh-boy-o," Aaron said in a tired tone with his elbows on the dinner table. I could tell he just wanted go lie down on the couch for an after-dinner nap.

"Oh, don't get me wrong. This will be fun," Jeffrey said, handing each of us two sheets of paper and a pair of scissors. "Okay, so here's what we're going to do. We each have a drawing of the inside of the *David B* on one sheet of paper. On the other sheet of paper there are four toilets, four sinks and four beds for you to cut out. They are all to scale, and the game is to see who can come up with the best arrangement for the cabins. The rules are that you can't put a sink or toilet under the beam shelf and that all doors must be able to open outward."

For an hour, the three of us worked our little beds, sinks and toilets like paper dolls. The hardest part was placing the toilets in each cabin. Just when I thought I had the perfect arrangement, I'd realize that there was not enough head room or space to sit down in the spot I had placed the toilet. Slowly, however, the layout of the cabins appeared on each of our sheets of

237

paper like the message from a Ouija board, and in the end all of us came up with almost exactly the same layout.

"I guess we're all winners," I said, when we'd agreed on the final design.

A few days before Sean was to start, he called to say that he had a friend who could use a few weeks of work as well, and, judging by the number of projects Jeffrey had described to him over the phone, we could use all the help we could get.

"I think that's a great idea. Let me just run it by Christine," Jeffrey said. I was sitting nearby and gave him the "okay" sign, and at the beginning of the next workweek, Sean arrived with his friend Chris. This brought to five the number of people staying in our tiny house.

The plywood for the cabins had arrived, and like everything else on the *David B*, it cost more than the ordinary kind. It was special marine plywood, and the price was about a hundred dollars per sheet, and we got somewhere around twenty sheets. I had to take a deep breath to let go of the anxiety I had when I opened the bill for the plywood. *It's okay, Christine, the money will come from somewhere, just believe. We may be going backwards now, but more reservations will start coming in and soon, things will change*, I told myself as I set the receipt in my overflowing inbox to deal with later.

Once Sean and Chris started working on the cabins, the momentum of the rebuild increased, and the fish hold seemed to magically transform from a dreary, dark space to a forest of plywood walls. The dark, dirty old fish hold was no longer a place where spiders might lurk. It was fast becoming a warm and welcoming place where you wanted to be. I felt confident that the *David B* would be finished in April, and I began to plan a launch party to celebrate the completion of the *David B* and the start of our business.

On July Fourth, twenty days into our journey, we saw our first ice. It was Independence Day, and like a fireworks display that starts slowly, our first iceberg was drifting all by itself in the middle of Stevens Passage. Jeffrey steered the *David B* close to it so we could get a better look. A flock of gulls stood on the berg and cautiously watched us approach. Then, as we neared, they all took off in unison, circling and calling in a cacophony of wing beats and cries.

The gulls flew toward a spot where three huge icebergs were fetched up on the shallow at the entrance to Holkham Bay. We, too, were going that direction. Jeffrey lined up between the green and red buoys that indicated where we could pass over the Tracy Arm bar. The water was flowing swiftly over the bar, and the buoys leaned with the current like little red- and green-hatted gnomes.

Once inside the bay, we toured around for a while, going from iceberg to iceberg, fascinated by their fantastic shapes. After a while, Jeffrey asked Aaron to go slow the engine down. "I want to stop and get some ice. It's the Fourth of July and we might need to celebrate when we drop the hook tonight."

After Aaron slowed the engine down, he came up on deck to help collect a small piece of ice. He grabbed a bucket with a long line attached to it as Jeffrey maneuvered near a patch of broken up bergie bits. "Don't try to get anything too big," he cautioned. "They always look smaller in the water than they really are. Remember the rule: you're only seeing the tip of the iceberg."

"Roger that," Aaron said, as he leaned over the lifelines to dip his bucket into the water.

"Did you get anything?" Sean asked as he took pictures of Aaron fishing for ice.

It took him several tries to catch the right one. "How about this?" he breathed in as he landed his bucket. Sean and I closed in to examine his catch. Its was unusually clear except for a point deep within it where the sunlight caught a hairline fracture and, like a tiny prism, radiated all the colors of the rainbow.

We motored to No Name Cove, a little bight near the mouth of Holkham Bay. It's the only really secure anchorage in Tracy Arm, so it was no surprise that there were several other boats at anchor when we arrived. We recognized one of them as a charter boat that we knew, the *Alaskan Song* from Bellingham.

Jeffrey anchored toward the outside of the cove. We had a glorious view of Holkham Bay with its icebergs, eagles, sea birds, and humpback whales. Sean was just getting our Fourth of July drinks ready when a Boston Whaler skiff loaded up with the crew and passengers from the *Alaskan Song* came over, dressed in their best pirate gear and ready to board.

"Ahoy, *David B*," the captain of the *Song* declared from his Boston Whaler.

"Ahoy," Sean said, holding his glass filled with glacier ice and whisky.

"Welcome to Alaska!" the captain said. "We've brought you a gift."

"Thanks," Jeffrey said, as he leaned over the rail to accept a bottle of champagne. "Did you guys go to the glacier today or are you going tomorrow?"

"We'll be underway at five a.m. tomorrow to get there early. I like to be the first one there."

"Do you have any ideas about what the ice conditions might be like?" Jeffrey asked.

The two captains talked shop for a bit, and then Jeffrey thought to ask if everyone would like to come aboard for a tour. Sean, Aaron, and I went to set up a couple of fenders for them to land up against, when all of a sudden a pasty-white body went flying past me and launched itself, screaming, over the top of the pirates' boat. I realized, as he was in mid-air, that it was Steven, who had suddenly decided to do a little swimming in the icy water. He landed a near-perfect cannonball just a couple of feet away from the surprised visitors.

"What the hell was that?" shouted someone from the Whaler.

"Oh, that was our naturalist," Sean said. "Yeah, he does that all the time."

"Oh my god, isn't the water cold?" someone else asked Steven as he swam.

"I like it. It feels great," he replied.

"Hey, Christine, can you go get the swim ladder so our polar bear can get back on board?" Jeffrey asked.

I was trying to decide whether Steven's actions were appropriate or not.

"Yeah, I'm on it."

We were boarded by the pirates and gave them a tour. While they were looking around, I opened the champagne.

They proposed a toast. "Welcome to Alaska!" their captain suggested. There was a round of glasses clinking and hurrahs.

"To Independence Day!" one of their passengers called out. While everyone cheered, it occurred to me that it really was *our* independence we were talking about: freedom from DEAD ENDs and NO OUTLETs and a life in a cubicle.

Then it was our turn. Jeffrey raised his glass and paused. The pilothouse went quiet.

"To the David B!"

CHAPTER 10

IT ALL SEEMED SO NATURAL

Time	Location	Wind	Baro	Depth	Remarks
0500	No Name Cove	Ø	102.6	37ft	Close - Sailon Humpbacks
0530	Under Way	Ø	1026		Calm Sunny Beautiful
1800	Secure Juneau	—Called Provisions		

M/V David B -- Ship's Log   Date: July 5 2006

WE GOT UNDERWAY EARLY the next morning to head up the fjord to North Sawyer Glacier. We didn't make it. The fjord that leads to the glacier was so choked with ice that we were forced to turn around. Sean was the most disappointed, and I was concerned that we might have the same problem when we returned with our passengers, since taking people to see a tidewater glacier was a big part of what we advertised.

We left Holkham Bay and turned north toward Juneau. All afternoon, we organized our tasks, making lists for what provisions we needed and for work that needed to be done on the engine. I was excited to get to Juneau. As we got closer, I strained to see the buildings in the distance. From the water, Juneau reminded me of Ketchikan; the town was built on the edge of a steep walled fjord and obscured by gleaming white cruise ships. Only the federal building could be seen above the wall of ships. The soundscape was also similar, but instead of nonstop floatplanes, it was the reverberation of helicopters that filled the air. They traveled in strings of three to five as they ferried the army of cruise-ship passengers on sightseeing excursions around Mendenhall glacier, the Juneau Ice field, and Taku Glacier. There were floatplanes coming and going as well. I imagined them as giant mosquitoes; their fuselage-bodies engorged with the weight of tourists in search of adventure. As each plane took off, it would come rushing toward us on what seemed like a collision course. At the last minute, the plane would lift its heavy load out of the water and just clear the *David B*. I waved to the passengers on the closest planes and could see energetic waves back from the small windows.

"Juneau Harbormaster, Juneau Harbormaster. This is the *David B*," Jeffrey called over the radio, keeping an eye out for floatplanes.

"*David B*, Juneau Harbormaster, go ahead," the voice over the radio sounded back.

"Yeah, Juneau Harbormaster, we're looking for moorage for two nights for a sixty-five-foot boat."

"Sixty-five feet for two nights. Roger that. Stand by while I see what we have," the harbormaster's voice crackled.

"Roger, *David B* standing by, on one-six and one-three," Jeffrey spoke into the radio.

Jeffrey went back to navigating through the busy channel. One by one, we began to gather in the pilothouse. Aaron had just gotten up from his nap and grabbed a bag of Cheetos before he sat down on the port-side seat.

"When we get into port, I'm gonna need to get some oil for the oil change," he said to Jeffrey while munching away.

"*David B*, Juneau Harbormaster," the voice was back on the radio, interrupting the oil change discussion.

"Juneau Harbormaster, *David B*," Jeffrey responded.

"*David B*, we've got a spot for you in the Aurora Boat Basin. Have you been here before?" the harbormaster asked.

"No, this is our first time to Juneau," Jeffrey said.

The harbormaster continued with the instructions on how to find our slip and which side we needed to tie up on.

When Jeffrey was done on the radio, he turned to us. "Hey, guys, tell me again, what's the height of the mast? There's a bridge coming up. Sean, can you look up the clearance? I'm sure we'll have plenty of space, but I think we should just double-check—and while you're at it, we'd better check the tide."

The *David B*'s Douglas fir mast stands forty-one feet above the waterline, and like most everything on the boat now, it was something we had replaced. Not long after we had taken the boat to Bellingham, Jeremy suggested that a friend of his on Lopez had two trees on his property that would make a good mast and boom. It sounded like a good idea, so we went back out to Lopez to do a little amateur logging. The trees were nice and straight and would have worked, but after felling them, we never had the time to get them to the boat. They either rotted in place or became firewood for someone.

In our search for another source for a mast, we discovered that a company in Bellingham makes utility poles. To ship the poles, they drive through town and past the entrance of Squalicum Harbor. One day, on our way home from the boat, we sat at a stop sign when a semi carrying utility poles drove by. "There's our mast!" Jeffrey said. "Why didn't I think of it before?" He was smiling and excited.

Our class-two utility pole arrived at the shipyard a couple of days before our second haul-out. To prepare the pole, Jeffrey and Aaron reshaped it to give it the right proportions. They varnished it and then attached the hardware for the stays, the wires that would hold the mast in place. While Jeffrey and Aaron worked on the mast, I began a search for a newly minted coin from 2006 to place under the mast. We needed the coin to keep a record of when the mast was replaced and to bring us good luck, following an ancient tradition started by Roman sailors. They believed that if the boat was ever lost and the sailors drowned, money placed under a mast could be used in the afterlife to pay the ferryman to cross the River Styx.

When we removed the old mast, we expected there to be several coins, but strangely, there was only one, and it was from 1986. We wondered what happened to the earlier coins and just assumed that Jeremy had either lost or kept them. We figured that the record of any new masts between 1929 and 1986 was lost to history. It never occurred to us that the reason for the missing coins was that there hadn't been a mast before 1986. Jeremy had put in the *David B's* first one when he moved the pilothouse aft to make it look like a halibut schooner.

It turned out that finding a coin from 2006 in March of 2006 was proving to be a difficult task. I'd been to several grocery stores to get rolls of quarters, and Jeffrey had been to the bank. We asked everyone we knew to search their pocket change for any coin from 2006. We were fast running out of time, and with only a few hours before we were to step the mast, Jeffrey thought of calling a coin store.

"So, you'll need to go over to the coin shop on Commercial Street on your way back from the hardware store. The woman there said that March is too early in the year for the new coins to be circulating, but they've got a 2006 silver dollar in stock."

"Great, I'll head over there."

When I got to the coin shop, I asked the woman about a 2006 coin. She said she had talked with Jeffrey and knew I would be coming in. When Jeffrey suggested I pick up the coin, I hadn't really thought about the fact that it was going to be a silver dollar. The saleswoman went into a back room and returned with a satchel that she carried very deliberately. Her body language suggested that our transaction would be expensive. She returned to the counter and opened the satchel. Carefully and purposely, she slid out a Navy-blue velvet jewelry box. She rotated it so that the hinge was facing her and opened the box slowly so I could anticipate the value of the coin inside. I leaned over the counter and inspected the shiny coin. It sparkled. In the light of the carefully placed halogen lights, the bald eagle and full moon scene almost seemed to leap off the coin.

"It's a very fine coin printed by the U.S. Mint. What do you think?" she asked.

"It's beautiful and the artwork has so much . . . uh, detail. How much is it?" I asked, just wanting to get the coin and get back to the boat.

"Only thirty-four dollars," she said. "A very good deal."

"Right, a very good deal indeed. If I were to spend this dollar, what could I get for it?" She didn't catch my humor and seemed annoyed with my question. She replied flatly that "as legal tender, it spends exactly as a dollar bill."

"Hmm, one dollar for thirty-four dollars. A steal for sure. I'll take it."

I reconciled with myself that on the nautical dollar scale, where every nautical dollar is worth a thousand regular dollars, this silver dollar was only thirty-four thousandths of a nautical dollar. I paid for the coin. My phone rang as I was getting into the car to head down to the shipyard. It was Jeffrey.

"Hi, where are you?" he asked.

"At the coin shop. Do you want to guess how much it costs?" I said.

"Hmmm, must have cost a lot if you're asking," he replied.

"Oh, yeah. It was thirty-four dollars, and if we tried to buy something with it, it would only be worth one dollar. You know, I'm so annoyed with how much everything is costing. I can't believe I just paid thirty-four dollars for a buck. It drives me bat-shit crazy. I don't care if it's the finest silver. It's still a frick'n dollar," I complained bitterly.

"Well, I see you're happy with your new purchase. Hurry back, because they're getting ready to bring the crane over to step the mast," he said.

When I arrived, Jeffrey and Aaron were both talking with the crane operator who was going to bring the mast from the other end of the shipyard to the *David B*. I walked up to them and proudly showed off the new coin.

"Wow, that's some nice bling. How much was it?" Aaron paused. "It's *really* shiny, isn't it?"

The silver dollar sparkled in its velvet case.

"Thirty-four dollars," Jeffrey and I said in unison.

"And it's really only worth a dollar? Dude, I think you just got hosed," Aaron laughed.

I climbed the ladder to the pilothouse and located the 1986 coin and a 1929 dime that we had purchased at an antique store. I wanted to take a picture of all the coins before taking them down below. Sean and Jack were at the base of the stairs, getting the mast step ready. I handed the coins to Sean, who approved of them. He set them in place and I took a few more pictures.

It was midafternoon, and the sky was overcast with thin clouds. The yellow crane drove over to the boat with the mast teeter-tottering on a wire line from its neck. When the operator pulled up alongside the boat, he set the mast down on some blocks next to the boat. Jeffrey spent a few more minutes talking with the crane operator. After a while, the operator got out of the cab, and they both walked over to the mast to monkey with the wires.

The mast was ready to go. Its top was finished and painted white, and the hardware that would hold the wire stays was on. The crane operator climbed back up into his cab and gave Jeffrey the thumbs-up. Jeffrey signaled that he was ready, too.

I stood back with my camera and watched as the crane operator moved into position. Jeffrey helped guide the mast as it lifted off the ground. Once everything looked like it was going according to plan, he ran up the ladder and over to the opening in the foredeck where the mast would go down. The operator carefully moved the whole crane back and extended the boom as the mast stood up vertically. Jeffrey, Aaron, and Jack were all on deck, ready to guide the mast into position. Jeffrey was in continuous contact with the crane operator using hand signals. He'd motion "a little left," "a little right," and "all good." Down below, Sean was ready to make sure that the bottom of the mast, or the key, as it is called, would slide perfectly into the step.

Watching the whole operation, I was mesmerized . Everything was choreographed perfectly. The mast was completely secure in less than fifteen minutes.

As we neared the bridge in Juneau, my heart raced. In less than ten minutes' time, we would be secure in Juneau.

"Aaron, do you want to slow us down a bit?' Jeffrey said. "Christine, Sean, looks like a starboard-side tie. Whenever you're ready to get the lines out, go ahead. Also, Christine, make sure you get a picture of us going under the bridge."

"Right, I'm on it," I said grabbing my camera. Sean left the pilothouse and walked up the deck. Steven followed to help.

I went out on deck to look up at the mast. The sky was bright blue, and the green pennant waved gently. I stood just in front of the pilothouse, watching the bridge get closer. I took a deep breath and momentarily held it. The bridge was like a gate, and once we passed under it, we would be at the destination we had worked so hard for over the last eight years. I thought back to the first day Jeffrey and I had gone to Lopez to see the *David B*. I thought about all the people who claimed we'd never finish restoring the boat. I felt proud as I watched the bridge near. We had started out with nothing but a rotten old wooden boat and a whole lot of ambition. *We did it, I can't believe it, we really did it,* I thought to myself, trying not to get all emotional and break out in tears.

I looked back at Jeffrey. He was leaning out the open pilothouse window with his left arm resting on the sill and his right hand on the wheel inside. He was smiling. The images of him backing the boat out of our slip on the first day of the journey came back to me. Over the last couple of weeks, he'd learned so many secrets that the *David B* had been waiting all these years to tell him. I thought about how many times I'd questioned our ability, and I thought of the boat itself: *You were right to pick us. Thank you for believing in us.*

Jeffrey caught me watching him. "We're almost there."

I smiled back to him, wanting to say something, but my eyes just welled up instead.

I lifted up my camera and took a couple of pictures as we went under the bridge and turned into the harbor.

Jeffrey maneuvered the *David B* into our assigned slip. Sean stepped off as we came alongside the dock and took a line from Aaron. "Spring's on!" Sean shouted, just like always.

There were people on the dock who had paused to watch us tie up. I handed Sean the bowline, and Aaron walked to the back of the boat to get the stern line. Jeffrey stood in the doorway of the pilothouse watching over us as we tied the lines. When we finished and he was satisfied, he looked over to Aaron. "Finished with engines," he said, and as soon as he spoke, a flannel-clad old man came over to ask questions about the boat, just as they did at every place we stopped.

Jeffrey beamed as he talked. I could see in his body language that he was proud of his boat, his crew, and his skill in running the boat. I sat down next to him on the pilothouse doorsill. I could hardly believe that we had just taken the seventy-seven-year-old *David B* on an eight-hundred-mile journey though the Inside Passage.

★

After a couple days of preparation and provisioning, we were ready to move the boat to the Intermediate Vessel Float in Juneau's downtown. The dock was full of tour boats similar to ours. As we approached the dock, the sound of our engine caused several crewmembers to stop their work and watch. When we were secure, a few came over to see the *David B*. They congratulated us on our rebuild and wished us well before going back to clean and provision their boats. I loved watching them work to get their boats ready. There was a feeling of community on the dock, and I looked forward to the years ahead when the *David B* would be full and we'd come to the dock regularly and be part of the scene.

We were almost ready for passengers, but we still needed to find firewood, which was turning out to be more difficult than we thought. We had enough on board to get us back down to Petersburg, but Jeffrey really wanted to load up with enough to get us back to Bellingham. Time was running short. Every time we left the boat, Jeffrey instructed us to look at people's footwear. If someone was wearing Xtratuf boots, it was likely that they were locals, not tourists, and we were to ask them about firewood. Still, no matter how many brown-booted people we talked to, no one seemed to know where to get firewood. Even though this part of Alaska seemed to be made entirely out of firewood, people cut, split, and hoarded their own wood and were not willing to part with their stashes.

While we had a lot of work to do, we still took a little time to do some sightseeing. The weather was nice, so we decided to take the tram up Mt. Roberts. The view from the top was beautiful, and we could see Gastineau Channel and the *David B* down below. It and all the other boats on the IVF were dwarfed by three huge cruise ships, also docked along the Juneau waterfront. Hiking the trails on Mt. Roberts felt good since we hadn't had much time for exercise. I also took lots of pictures of high elevation wildflowers along the trail. When we returned to the tram, we were lucky enough to see a black bear wandering in the underbrush below.

The next morning, we needed to take Sean to the airport. His time with us on the *David B* was over, and by nightfall he'd be in Seattle. But first, we really wanted Sean to see a glacier up close while he was in Alaska. We got up early, picked up some coffee and bagels, then went to Mendenhall Glacier. When we got there, the parking lot was empty, and since there weren't any cruise ships in town yet, the park and the interpretative center were quiet.

The center is perched on a rise next to a lake about a mile from the glacier. Mendenhall's face is a mile-and-a-half-wide wall that stands a hundred feet above the lake. We walked around some of the trails and spent time watching the glacier. Hikers were traversing the glacier, and from our vantage point, they seemed so small. While we watched the glacier, we talked to Sean about how much his help over the last few months meant to us and told him we couldn't have made it to Juneau without him. He seemed touched. He was, however, happy to be going home and to be rid of Steven, who had kept to himself and hadn't participated in any of the crew activities for the last couple of days.

We went back to the car to take Sean to the airport. We said our good-byes and watched Sean walk through the double doors. Jeffrey was still concerned that we didn't have any firewood yet, and we talked about calling some friends in Petersburg to see if they could line up some wood for us. As I drove into the parking lot for the IVF, Jeffrey saw the harbormaster. "Hey, I'm going to see if he knows where to get some wood. What are you doing next?"

"I've got an appointment with the woman from a fishing boat who sells salmon and halibut out of her cold-storage unit. I guess it's near Costco, so I'll stop there and the Alaska and Proud grocery store as well. I also want to stop at Rainbow Foods to see what their fruits, veggies, and cheeses are like. I guess I'll be back to the boat sometime after lunch."

I pulled out of the parking lot and had been gone for about five minutes when Jeffrey called.

"Hey, can you go by the liquor store called Crate and Barrel near Western Auto and Marine and see if there's a guy named Tattoo? He sells firewood."

"Really? That's awesome. I'm almost there. I'll let you know what I find out."

When I got there, it wasn't open. I looked around the dirt parking lot and noticed a pile of wood, some rounds and some split. There was a drive-thru coffee stand nearby, so I decided that a dollar-fifty cup of coffee would be a good way to find out if the pile of wood belonged to Tattoo.

I drove up to the coffee stand and rolled down the car window. A young woman stuck her head out of the stand's window and asked what I wanted.

"Tall drip, please," I ordered. "And, also, do you know if there's a guy named Tattoo who owns that woodpile?"

"Room for cream?" She asked, walking away from the window a step or two. "Oh yeah, the woodpile's Tattoo's. He chops wood for people all the time. Come back when the liquor store's open. He's usually there," she said.

Once I pulled away from the coffee stand I stopped and called Jeffrey.

"I found Tattoo. You'll want to call the Crate and Barrel after eleven and ask for him. He's got a big pile of wood here. I got the scoop from the coffee girl."

Jeffrey took down the information and said he'd try calling him.

I spent a couple more hours provisioning. When I got back to the boat, I asked Jeffrey if he had gotten hold of Tattoo. He hadn't, but the person who answered the phone at the liquor store promised to give him the message. Later, I heard Jeffrey's phone ring. It was Tattoo. I'd forgotten all about wood and was thinking about getting started on dinner. I listened to the conversation, and when Jeffrey hung up the phone he was excited. Tattoo was going to pick him up to go to his place and load some wood.

"That's awesome, but I think you should take Aaron with you. They guy's name is Tattoo, after all," I said.

At eight forty-five Tattoo came down to the dock. He was very short, with curly dark hair, and he wore tall leather boots and pants that were torn off to mid-calf, like a logger's. I knew immediately where his nickname had come from, but instead of a fine pressed white tuxedo, he was the woodsman version of the *Fantasy Island* character.

Jeffrey gave Tattoo a quick tour of the boat and then called Aaron out of the engine room. The three of them left. I really wondered if it was a good idea. He seemed nice enough, so I figured that there was probably no harm. Besides, they were just going out to the parking lot by the marine store. If anything went wrong, both Jeffrey and Aaron had cell phones.

They were gone until ten-thirty or so. During that time, I finished cleaning up the boat with Steven's help and made some bread and soup while we waited. When the guys came back, we filled up dock carts, handed wood over the rail, and piled it up into the galley. Jeffrey went down into the engine room, and we passed it down to him. When we finished, we had a full wood bin that would last us until we got to Ketchikan and probably a few days more. We would need to find wood again, but for now we were full.

We thanked Tattoo for helping us. I gave him a loaf of bread, and Jeffrey gave him some cash. It was almost eleven p.m.

After Tattoo left, Jeffrey and Aaron couldn't wait to tell the story of their adventure with him.

"So," Jeffrey began, "first there was his truck. You saw it. Mid-eighties-something and mostly broken. Anyway, after Aaron and I got in and he started it up, he had the radio cranked up with Loverboy. We couldn't even talk. Then, when Tattoo asked us asked a question, he'd turn down the tunes just long enough for the answer. He had been to Bellingham and was really excited about hanging out on Railroad Avenue."

Aaron jumped in. "He wanted to know if people still hung out there."

"He wanted to hear about what it was like now," Jeffrey said. "Then, he cranked the radio back up. He kept doing radio up, radio down, question, radio up, radio down, question, all the way to his place."

"Yeah, but the best part was his brakes." Aaron snorted, laughing. "When we would come to a stoplight, Tattoo would start pumping the brakes. I thought *for sure* we'd go right though that one red light, but he just turned the radio down and started talking about how he used to live in Olympia and how he's a third generation woodcutter while he pumped."

According to Jeffrey and Aaron, Tattoo was a master wood splitter. He worked with almost unbelievable speed. His hand came down on each piece of wood just after the ax split it, to keep it standing for the next chop. He'd pick up another piece, and "Whack!" the wood would just fall apart. "A three-fer," he'd occasionally say if the wood he was splitting came apart in three pieces.

"Tattoo said he'd split about ten thousand cords of wood since he moved to Juneau," Jeffrey said.

"Then he wanted us to see his place," Aaron said. "It was back behind the liquor store and I shit you not"—he started laughing—"it was a camper, the kind of camper that sits on a pickup truck. Only there wasn't a pickup underneath. It was sitting on the ground."

"And he also had a fire pit with some lawn chairs around it," Jeffrey added. "The whole ground around the fire pit was a like a mat of cigarette butts, inches deep."

Jeffrey began laughing so hard that he had trouble getting the rest of the story out. Both his and Aaron's faces were turning red as they talked about their tour of Tattoo's camper.

"So, he wanted to show off the Christmas lights that he'd strung up around the camper, and he very proudly took the plug for the lights and began to plug them into an extension cord that ran from who-knows-where, and as he did, it caught fire. Flames actually shot out of the extension cord," Jeffrey said. "What was really surprising was how calm he was about it."

"Yeah, didn't he say something like, 'Well, that wasn't supposed to happen,'" Aaron said. "Then he wanted to give us a fire ax for the boat."

"So, did he give you one?" I asked.

"Yeah. It's on the back deck. It's a nice traditional one. Tattoo said we shouldn't be without one, so he threw it in for free," Jeffrey said.

"Wow, that was nice of him. It's so cool how many people see the boat and want to do something for it. He doesn't have much, but he gave us something that he thought we could use." I thought about the people who saw what we were doing and helped in some way. *It's touching every time, no matter the size of the contribution. Boats, and especially wooden boats, seem to have a charisma that draws people to them. I'm so amazed by what people will do for a boat.*

☆

Everything was ready. The wood bin was full, the groceries were stowed, and the staterooms were made up. The chrome on the stove sparkled, and the galley brass was polished.

I was dead tired but too excited to go to bed, so I poured myself a glass of wine and joined Jeffrey and Aaron on the bridge deck. Jeffrey was tidying up a few last-minute details. I sat down on the starboard side seat and stared out at the now-empty cruise ship dock in front of us. I couldn't get out of my mind how thoughtful it was of Tattoo to give us a fire ax. His generosity reminded me of all the people we had invited to our launch party three months earlier. A hundred and fifty or more people who had in some way contributed to the transformation of the *David B* came to celebrate the boat's new life.

We had rented the Squalicum Boathouse, a small reception hall with a dock in a park. Jeffrey, Aaron, and Sean moved the *David B* to the dock while I set up tables and chairs and worked with the caterer. Once everything was decorated, I walked across the grassy space between the boathouse and the dock. It was such a contrast, seeing the *David B* for the first time that day compared to the first time we saw it on Lopez Island, so many years earlier. After eight years of work, the boat had been transformed from a dying hulk to a beautiful work of art that was filled with countless hours of labor and love. Sean had brought a set of signal flags and they were strung from the bow to the stern. It was a cool, cloudy April day, and the brightly colored flags were brilliant against the grey overcast. The boat was beautiful.

Flying from the top of the mast was a surprise that Jeffrey had made for me: a green pennant with white letters that read "DAVID B." I stopped halfway across the lawn when I noticed it. My emotions welled up inside me, and I stood there with happy tears, hoping no one would notice.

✯

"It was a lot like our wedding in some ways," I said aloud, as I snapped out of my reflection.

"Huh? What was?" Jeffrey answered back as he polished the brass shifter handle.

"You know, the launching party."

"Oh, yeah. That was a big day. We were lucky to pull the whole thing off. Do you remember how ticked off Sean was the night before, trying to get the skylight installed, and how late we had to stay up?"

"And remember how your sister and parents walked down the dock with the doors for the cabins, only to have walk them back up the dock once we realized that the paint on them hadn't dried?" I laughed.

"Right, and then Aaron almost didn't make it because he and his brother went bar hopping late that night and slept at some random person's house. I was sure when he called, ten minutes before we needed to move the boat, that he was in jail."

"Yeah, and how many people were at the house the night before?" I asked, trying to mentally count the number of people camped out in sleeping bags on the floor of our tiny house.

"Well, there was Danny and his girlfriend, Aaron's friend Andrea, Sean, and Jean . . ." Jeffrey stated counting off people.

"And don't forget your sister was sleeping under the dining room table and my mom on the kitchen floor," I said.

"I still love it that we didn't have any sinks yet in the cabins and the toilets were all just set in place with no plumbing. You know, maybe the best thing about the launching party was standing up on deck with you, Aaron, and my parents," Jeffrey said, "and looking at everyone who came to the party. It was so fun to hand the bottle of champagne to my mom and let her break it over the bow."

Jeffrey paused, and Aaron, who had been sitting on the other side of the bridge deck quietly reading, broke in. "Yeah, and she just crushed the shit out of that bottle! There's still bits of green glass up there. For someone who's as sweet as your mom, she really knows how to throw her weight into her swing."

We all laughed, and Jeffrey said, "She was really worried that she wouldn't break it on the first swing, and that would bring us bad luck."

"Well, judging by the weather and how things have been going so far, it seems like—for now, anyhow —we have luck on our side." I smiled and knocked on the wooden table.

I woke up the next morning minutes before my alarm went off. I was anxious. In four hours, we would meet our first passengers. The boat was ready. I was ready. Jeffrey seemed to be ready. I hoped that Steven was ready. The seventy-two bottles of wine I had arranged for the trip were ready. What could possibly go wrong? I smiled to myself as I thought up unlikely scenarios of our passengers disliking my cooking, the boat, or us. All of my e-mails back and forth indicated that they would be fun and interesting people to spend eight days with.

By 0830, the sour-cream blueberry muffins were out of the oven, and I set them in a basket. I'd also carefully sliced and arranged a plate of fruit. My bread dough was rising, and the coffee was made. While I waited and watched for our passengers, I nervously cleaned the galley and rearranged pillows in the settee. I was thankful when the engineer from another boat came over to look at our engine. It provided a nice distraction. I felt a little fidgety, listening to Jeffrey and Aaron talk with him before they went down to the engine room. While they talked, I folded and refolded the same bar towel. I stood in front of the warm wood stove. The clouds outside were low and there was a heavy mist in the air. It was the kind of rain that soaks you to the bone without your knowing it.

"Ok, guys, passengers are arriving in fifteen minutes," Jeffrey said, climbing out of the engine room. "I think we're ready to go. As soon as they're on and they've gotten their things stowed, I'll do a safety talk and orientation. Then we can get out of here."

In a few minutes, I saw four people walking down the dock pulling large suitcases. I felt my heart race and looked over to Jeffrey and said, "I think they're here."

We didn't need to say anything to each other as we both instinctively stepped out of the pilothouse and began to walk toward our passengers. Jeffrey greeted the foursome.

"Hi, I'm Jeffrey. You guys look like you're looking for the *David B.*"

"We are. I'm Robert. This is my wife, Meredith, and our friends Stephen and Stephanie." Robert shook Jeffrey's hand, then came over to me. I introduced myself, and he gave me a hug and a kiss on the cheek. I relaxed and knew that it was going to be a good week.

We welcomed them aboard and showed them around the boat. Jeffrey gave his first safety talk and we prepared to get underway. Aaron went down into the engine room. In a few moments, the sound of the engine filled the air. People on the dock stopped to watch. Jeffrey stood in the doorway of the pilothouse.

"Ready for the bowline," he said, with his usual grin.

It was the start of a new journey. The flutter of excitement from departing on another trip and living the life I had made for myself outweighed the hint of apprehension. I knew what to do, and that filled me with a certain calm as Jeffrey said those words.

As I climbed aboard, I waved to the people gathered on the dock. I closed the gate and put away the fenders, then coiled up the lines. It began to rain. My hands were cold and wet, but I felt warmth inside me as I listened to the rise and fall of Jeffrey's voice, the laughter, and the Australian accents. They were gathered on the bridge deck. It all seemed so natural, as if we had always been running this boat—but no, I had to remind myself, this was our first trip. This was our beginning.

M/V David B -- Ship's Log

Date: 09 July 06

Time	Location	Wind	Baro	Depth	Remarks
	AT JUNEAU DOCK		1010	LT	RAIN / OVERCAST
1035	SAFETY ORIENTATION - 4 PASSENGERS ABOARD / 4 CREW				
1050	UNDERWAY FROM JUNEAU				

PHOTO ALBUMS

PHOTOS OF
REBUILDING THE DAVID B

Left: The *David B* moored at Lopez Island in May 1998.

Below: The condtion of the stern and aft end of the pilothouse in May 1998.

The plywood box and framework supporting the pilothouse when Christine and Jeffrey purchased the boat.

The *David B*'s original Shipmate wood cookstove.

Above: The engine room with the 3-cylinder Washington-Estep engine. Beyond the engine is a cutout in the bulkhead that led into the area that Jeremy called the fish hold.

Left: The swing float that Jeremy built to get to where the *David B* was moored.

Left: Christine works with a Skilsaw to remove the *David B's* foredeck. June 1998.

Above: Jeffrey cleaning the anchor chain locker.

Left: Christine's sister, Leigh, the first person who volunteered on the *David B.*

Christine, in the galley, trying on a mock-up of the wedding dress that her mom, Carol, designed.

Jeffrey planing deck beams, summer of 1998.

Carol photographs Rick, Jeffrey, Ken, and Steve as they move a plank from Steve's BMW to the *David B*.

Left: The completed foredeck.

Below: The last day the *David B* was at Lopez Island. Note the crane in the background that Jeffrey and Michael used to lift the windlass onto the boat.

Michael manually shifting the engine while underway from Lopez Island. February 1999.

The *Chief Kwina* towing the *David B* to Bellingham. February 1999.

Jeffrey removing the rotten beam shelf. Winter 2000.

Tom building the trunk cabin framework. Winter 2000.

The interior of the boat after the removal of the main bulkhead. Winter 2000.

One of many deliveries of new wood for the boat.

The *David B* in the slings of the TraveLift in December 2004.

Jeffrey scraping mussels and barnacles from the rudder just after hauling out.

The stern of the boat after it was blocked up in the shipyard.

All that remained after rotten wood was removed from the stern, January 2005.

Jeffrey and Greg examine the rim log around the back of the boat.

Aaron takes a brief break after putting up several new planks. March 2005.

Jeffrey (top) prepares to remove a plank from the steam box and Aaron (bottom) uses a jack stand to hold a new plank in place so it can be fastened to the boat. March 2005.

Christine fills the seams with Portland cement after all the planks were hung and caulked. April 2005

A few days before the *David B* went back in the water, May 2005.

Greg, Jeffrey, Dan, Jon-Paul, and Aaron admire the *David B* on the night before launching. May 2005.

The interior of the boat with a new bulkhead. Spring 2006.

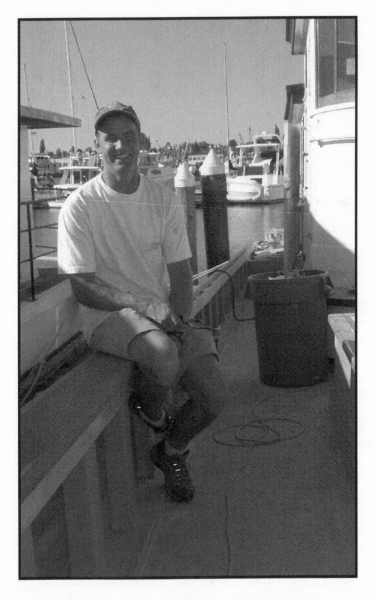

Jeffrey poses on the *David B's* not-yet-completed rail cap.
Summer 2005.

Left: Sean in early 2006, building the cabins. He later sailed as the *David B's* mate.

Below: Aaron laying new flooring the in the fish hold where the new cabins were built. Spring 2006.

Left: Coins placed under the new mast for good luck. They are from 1929, 1986, and 2006.

Below: Installing new mast in the spring of 2006.

Right: The new Heartland wood cookstove.

Below: Greg building the table for the galley. The post in the middle of the table surrounds the exhaust pipe from the engine.

Above: The finished galley in 2006 with the dining table and the Sweetheart cookstove. Below: The bridge deck, looking up from the galley.

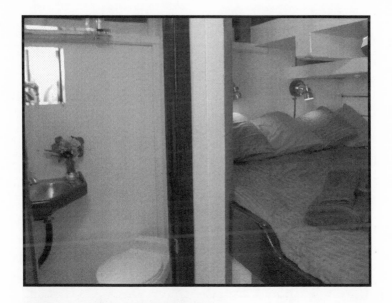

Above: The Sockeye stateroom and private head finished in time for the launching part

Left: The forward head with its cast-iron bathtub and shower. Spring 2006.

The *David B* on April 15, 2006, dressed up with signal flags for her Launching Day Party.

PHOTOS
UNDERWAY FOR JUNEAU

Above: The *David B* in Bellingham Bay, underway for Alaska. Photo by Cathy Wade.

Approaching Dodd Narrows.
Photo By Sean Bull

Christine enjoying the warm deck while cruising through
Homfray Channel.

Christine's view from her favorite spot to relax in the sun on
the foredeck.

A southbound cruise ship in Johnstone Strait.

Aaron naps in his favorite comfortable spot on the *David B.*

Above: Christine making bread. Below: Cruising through Fry Pan Bay. Photos by Sean Bull.

Above: Bottleneck Inlet.

Left: The *David B* nearing the Canada-United States Border northbound for Alaska.
Photos by Sean Bull.

Top: Sean and Steven point out whales feeding near the *David B* in Alaska. Below: Humpback fluke in Frederick Sound, Alaska. Photo by Sean Bull

Above: Holkham Bay ice.

Right: Steven (shirtless), just after cannonballing into the water next to a visiting skiff of well-wishers, No Name Cove, Alaska. Photo by Sean Bull

Above: Tracy Arm,
Holkham Bay,
Alaska.

Left:
Passing under the
bridge, Juneau,
Alaska.

Above: The crew taking some time off in Juneau for a little sightseeing before getting the boat ready for the first passengers. Below: Christine, Jeffrey, and Sean at Mendenhall glacier.

To see more pictures visit: MoreFasterBackwards.com/photos/

ABOUT THE AUTHOR

Christine Smith lives in Bellingham, Washington, with her husband, Jeffrey, and their two cats, Harriet and Oswald. When not working on the *David B*, she can be found running on local trails, skiing, bird watching, and baking bread.

To contact the author, e-mail her at christine@morebasterbackwards.com

For information on, or to book a cruise aboard the *David B* visit NWNavigation.com or call 877-670-7863.

Made in the USA
Charleston, SC
09 October 2012